Puddings

THE AUSTRALIAN
Women's Weekly

Puddings

acp
books

CONTENTS

INTRODUCTION 6

FRUIT & NUT PUDDINGS 8

MILK PUDDINGS 104

STEAMED PUDDINGS 168

MOUSSES 192

SELF-SAUCING PUDDINGS 246

SOUFFLES 274

DESSERT CAKES 318

GLOSSARY 386

INDEX 392

CONVERSION CHART 399

SWEET MEMORIES

Most of us have sweet memories of puddings from our childhood: bread and butter pudding at grandma's house or sticky date pudding on a dreary Sunday afternoon. That's why we pounce on them whenever we see them on restaurant menus. There are plenty of them in this book but there are also modern puddings such as tiramisu that we had never heard of when we were children (unless our parents were Italian) and fig and brioche pudding – a delicious and elegant French concoction.

We've stretched the meaning of pudding to include such things as crème caramel and panna cotta, usually referred to as desserts. You'll also find mousses, soufflés, dessert cakes and crumbles.

Fruit & nut puddings include Christmas puddings and sticky date puddings as well as berry crumble and chocolate pecan pudding.

Milk puddings naturally contain rice puddings, bread and butter puddings and crème caramel, as well as ice-cream puddings.

Steamed puddings include the famous college pudding and ginger pudding in among recipes for steamed chocolate puddings and a delicious steamed date pudding.

Mousses are a perennial favourite, especially chocolate mousse with all its variations. Here there are also berry mousse, mango mousse, even piña colada mousse.

Self-saucing puddings are those magical puddings that, once turned out, have a sweet sauce that runs over the top; most famous of all is lemon delicious.

Soufflés are renowned for being difficult to make and temperamental. This is simply not true. Follow the instructions and you'll be amazed at how easy it is to truly impress.

Dessert cakes are richer than most other cakes — they are often served with a syrup or a sauce and are usually accompanied with cream or ice-cream.

FRUIT & NUT
PUDDINGS

classic boiled christmas pudding

4 cups (750g) mixed dried fruit
1⅓ cups (185g) seeded dried
  dates, chopped coarsely
1¼ cups (185g) raisins,
  chopped coarsely
1½ cups (375ml) water
¾ cup (165g) caster sugar
1 cup (200g) firmly packed
  brown sugar
250g butter, chopped
1½ teaspoons bicarbonate of soda

3 eggs, beaten lightly
¼ cup (60ml) dark rum
3 cups (210g) firmly packed
  fresh white breadcrumbs
1¾ cups (260g) plain flour
2 teaspoons mixed spice
1 teaspoon ground cinnamon
60cm square calico
⅓ cup (50g) plain flour, extra
2.5m kitchen string

1 Stir fruit, the water, sugars and butter in large saucepan over heat until sugar dissolves; bring to the boil. Simmer, 8 minutes. Stir in soda; cool.

2 Stir in egg, rum, breadcrumbs and sifted flour and spices.

3 Fill a large boiler three-quarters full of hot water, cover; bring to the boil. Have string and extra flour ready. Wearing thick rubber gloves, drop pudding cloth in boiling water; squeeze excess water from cloth. Spread hot cloth on bench, rub extra flour onto cloth 40cm in diameter, leaving flour a little thicker in centre.

4 Place pudding mixture in centre of cloth. Tie cloth tightly with string as close to mixture as possible. Knot two pairs of corners together.

5 Lower pudding into boiling water. Cover with tight lid; boil 6 hours, replenishing water as necessary to maintain water level.

6 Lift pudding from water; place in large colander; cut string, carefully peel back cloth. Turn pudding onto a plate; carefully peel away cloth, cool. Stand 20 minutes before serving.

prep + cook time 6 hours 30 minutes (+ cooling and standing)
serves 12
tips You'll need a 60cm square of unbleached calico for the pudding cloth. If the calico hasn't been used before, start with an 80cm square of calico, soak in cold water overnight. Next day, boil it for 20 minutes, rinse in cold water and cut to a 60cm square.
To store pudding, we prefer to remove the cloth rather than hanging the pudding, as mould can form in our climate. After removing cloth, allow pudding to come to room temperature; wrap in plastic wrap and seal tightly in a freezer bag or airtight container, and refrigerate for up to two months.

almond and raspberry frozen puddings

3 eggs
⅓ cup (75g) caster sugar
600ml thickened cream
1 teaspoon vanilla extract
1 tablespoon framboise or kirsch (optional)
⅓ cup (50g) vienna almonds, chopped coarsely
⅔ cup (70g) frozen raspberries
200g white eating chocolate, melted
fresh raspberries, for serving

1 Beat eggs and sugar in small bowl with electric mixer about 5 minutes or until mixture is very pale and fluffy. Transfer to large bowl.
2 Beat cream, extract and liqueur in small bowl with electric mixer until soft peaks form. Gently fold cream mixture into egg mixture with nuts and frozen raspberries.
3 Divide mixture among eight ¾-cup (180ml) moulds. Cover; freeze overnight or until firm.
4 Wipe moulds with a hot damp cloth and turn out onto serving plates. Spoon melted chocolate over top; serve with raspberries.

prep time 25 minutes (+ freezing) **serves** 8
tips Vienna almonds (candied or glazed) are available from delicatessens, health food stores and good confectionary shops. This recipe can be made a week ahead.

apple and marmalade streusel pudding

20g butter
4 medium apples (600g), peeled, cored, sliced thinly
2 tablespoons water
1 tablespoon caster sugar
½ cup (170g) orange marmalade
streusel
½ cup (75g) plain flour
¼ cup (35g) self-raising flour
⅓ cup (75g) firmly packed brown sugar
½ teaspoon ground cinnamon
100g butter, chopped

1 Make streusel.
2 Preheat oven to 200°C/180°C fan-forced. Grease four ¾-cup (180ml) ovenproof dishes.
3 Melt butter in medium frying pan; cook apple, the water and sugar, stirring, about 10 minutes or until apple is tender. Stir in marmalade. Divide mixture among dishes.
4 Coarsely grate streusel onto baking paper; sprinkle over apple mixture.
5 Bake pudding about 20 minutes or until browned lightly.
streusel Blend or process all ingredients until combined. Roll into a ball; wrap in plastic. Freeze dough about 1 hour or until firm.

prep + cook time 40 minutes (+ freezing) **serves** 4
tip Streusel can be frozen for up to one week. The fruit mixture can be cooked and stored, covered, in the refrigerator overnight.

summer pudding

3 eggs
½ cup (110g) caster sugar
1 tablespoon cornflour
¾ cup (110g) self-raising flour
1 teaspoon butter
¼ cup (60ml) boiling water

⅓ cup (75g) caster sugar, extra
½ cup (125ml) water
2 cups (300g) frozen blackberries
3⅓ cups (500g) frozen
  mixed berries
¼ cup (80g) blackberry jam

1 Preheat oven to 180°C/160°C fan-forced. Grease 25cm x 30cm swiss roll pan; line base with baking paper, extending paper 5cm over long sides.

2 Beat eggs in small bowl with electric mixer until thick and creamy. Gradually add sugar, beating until sugar dissolves; transfer mixture to large bowl.

3 Fold triple-sifted flours into egg mixture. Pour combined butter and boiling water down side of bowl; fold into egg mixture. Spread mixture into pan; bake 15 minutes. Cool in pan.

4 Meanwhile, combine extra sugar and the water in medium saucepan; bring to the boil. Stir in berries; return to the boil. Reduce heat; simmer, uncovered, until berries soften. Strain over medium bowl; reserve syrup and berries separately.

5 Turn cake onto board. Line 1.25-litre (5-cup) pudding basin with plastic wrap, extending wrap 10cm over side of basin. Cut circle slightly smaller than top edge of basin from cake using tip of sharp knife; cut second circle exact size of base of basin from cake. Cut remaining cake into 10cm long strips.

6 Place small cake circle in base of basin and use cake strips to line side of basin. Pour ⅔ cup of the reserved syrup into small jug; reserve. Fill basin with berries; cover with remaining syrup, top with large cake circle. Cover pudding with overhanging plastic wrap, weight pudding with saucer; refrigerate 3 hours or overnight.

7 Stir jam and 2 tablespoons of the reserved syrup in small saucepan until heated through. Turn pudding onto serving plate; brush with remaining reserved syrup then jam mixture. Serve with whipped cream.

prep + cook time 45 minutes (+ refrigeration) **serves** 6

lemon meringue pudding

200g bought sponge cake
1¾ cups (430ml) cream
1 teaspoon vanilla extract
1 teaspoon finely grated lemon rind
⅓ cup (80ml) lemon juice
6 eggs
¾ cup (165g) caster sugar
280g jar lemon butter

meringue topping
3 egg whites
¾ cup (165g) caster sugar
1 tablespoon caster sugar, extra
yellow food colouring

1 Preheat oven to 160°C/140°C fan-forced. Grease round 2-litre (8-cup) ovenproof dish.
2 Cut sponge cake into 3cm pieces; place pieces randomly in dish. Combine cream, extract, rind and juice in small saucepan over low heat, stirring until hot.
3 Whisk eggs and sugar in large bowl until combined. Whisking constantly, pour hot cream mixture into egg mixture; pour into dish over sponge cake.
4 Bake pudding 45 minutes; remove from oven. Increase oven temperature to 180°C/160°C fan-forced.
5 Cool pudding for 10 minutes, then, using rubber spatula, carefully spread lemon butter over surface.
6 Make meringue topping. Spoon topping over pudding to completely cover surface; sprinkle yellow sugar evenly over meringue.
7 Bake pudding about 15 minutes or until browned lightly. Serve hot with cream or ice-cream.
meringue topping Beat egg whites in small bowl with electric mixer until soft peaks form; add sugar, a tablespoon at a time, beating until sugar dissolves between additions. Tint extra sugar with a little yellow colouring in small bowl.

prep + cook time 1 hour 15 minutes **serves** 8
tips You can buy a sponge cake at most supermarkets. You need one lemon for the juice and the rind.

toffee date and ginger puddings

½ cup (115g) finely chopped glacé ginger
½ cup (60g) finely chopped roasted walnuts
1 cup (140g) seeded dried dates
¾ cup (180ml) water
1 teaspoon bicarbonate of soda
50g butter, chopped coarsely
½ cup (110g) firmly packed brown sugar
2 eggs
¾ cup (110g) self-raising flour
1 teaspoon ground ginger
ginger butterscotch sauce
½ cup (110g) firmly packed brown sugar
⅔ cup (160ml) cream
100g butter, chopped coarsely
½ teaspoon ground ginger

1 Preheat oven to 160°C/140°C fan-forced. Grease six-hole ¾-cup (180ml) texas muffin pan; line bases with baking paper.
2 Combine glacé ginger and nuts in small bowl; sprinkle mixture over bases of pan holes.
3 Combine dates and the water in small saucepan; bring to the boil. Remove from heat; stir in soda. Stand 5 minutes.
4 Blend or process date mixture with butter and sugar until smooth. Add eggs, flour and ground ginger; process until combined. Pour mixture into pan holes.
5 Bake puddings about 30 minutes. Stand 5 minutes; turn onto wire rack to cool 5 minutes.
6 Meanwhile, make ginger butterscotch sauce.
7 Serve warm puddings drizzled with ginger butterscotch sauce.
ginger butterscotch sauce Stir ingredients in small saucepan over low heat until smooth. Simmer, uncovered, 5 minutes.

prep + cook time 45 minutes **serves** 6

chocolate sticky date pudding

1½ cups (240g) seeded
  chopped dates
1¾ cups (430ml) water
1 teaspoon bicarbonate of soda
80g of butter, chopped
⅔ cup (150g) caster sugar
2 eggs
1 cup (150g) self-raising flour
⅓ cup (35g) cocoa powder
⅔ cups (70g) pecans, roasted,
  chopped coarsely

butterscotch sauce
1¼ cups (250g) firmly packed
  brown sugar
80g butter
300ml thickened cream

1 Preheat oven to 180°C/160°C fan-forced. Grease deep 22cm-round cake pan; line base with baking paper.

2 Combine dates and the water in small saucepan; bring to the boil. Remove from heat; stir in soda. Stand 5 minutes. Blend or process date mixture until smooth.

3 Beat butter and sugar in small bowl with electric mixer until combined. Beat in eggs, one at a time. Transfer mixture to large bowl. Fold in sifted flour and cocoa; stir in nuts and warm date mixture, in two batches. Pour mixture into pan.

4 Bake pudding about 1 hour. Stand in pan 10 minutes before turning onto serving plate.

5 Meanwhile, make butterscotch sauce.

6 Serve pudding with hot sauce and whipped cream, if you like.

butterscotch sauce Stir all ingredients in medium pan over heat, without boiling, until sugar is dissolved. Simmer, without stirring, 3 minutes.

prep + cook time 1 hour 30 minutes **serves** 10

ginger sticky date pudding

1 cup (140g) seeded dried dates
¼ cup (55g) glacé ginger
1 teaspoon bicarbonate of soda
1 cup (250ml) boiling water
50g butter, chopped
½ cup (110g) firmly packed brown sugar
2 eggs
1 cup (150g) self-raising flour
1 teaspoon ground ginger
butterscotch sauce
300ml cream
¾ cup (165g) firmly packed brown sugar
75g butter, chopped

1 Preheat oven to 200°C/180°C fan-forced. Grease deep 20cm-round cake pan; line base with baking paper.
2 Combine dates, ginger, soda and the water in food processor; stand 5 minutes then add butter and sugar. Process until mixture is almost smooth. Add eggs, flour and ginger; process until combined. Pour mixture into pan.
3 Bake pudding about 45 minutes. Stand in pan 10 minutes before turning onto serving plate.
4 Meanwhile, make butterscotch sauce.
5 Serve pudding warm with sauce.
butterscotch sauce Stir ingredients in medium saucepan over low heat until sauce is smooth.

prep + cook time 1 hour **serves** 8

plum clafoutis

10 small plums (750g), halved, seeded
1 cinnamon stick, halved
¼ cup (60ml) water
¼ cup (55g) brown sugar
⅔ cup (160ml) milk
⅔ cup (160ml) cream
1 teaspoon vanilla extract
4 eggs
½ cup (110g) caster sugar
¼ cup (35g) plain flour

1 Preheat oven to 200°C/180°C fan-forced. Grease shallow 2.5-litre (10-cup) ovenproof dish.
2 Place plums in medium baking dish with cinnamon and the water; sprinkle with brown sugar. Cook about 15 minutes or until plums soften.
3 Remove cinnamon from dish and add to medium saucepan with milk, cream and extract; bring to the boil. Cool; remove cinnamon stick.
4 Whisk eggs and caster sugar in medium bowl until light and frothy; whisk in flour then whisk mixture into cream mixture.
5 Place drained plums in shallow ovenproof dish; pour cream mixture over plums.
6 Bake clafoutis about 30 minutes or until browned lightly. Serve dusted with icing sugar.

prep + cook time 1 hour (+ cooling) **serves** 6
tip If plums are not in season, use a 1kg jar of whole plums. Drain, halve and seed them before using.

fig and brioche pudding

1½ cups (375ml) milk
600ml cream
1 cinnamon stick
1 vanilla bean
¼ cup (90g) honey
4 eggs
2 small brioche (200g)
3 medium fresh figs (180g)
1 tablespoon demerara sugar

1 Preheat oven to 180°C/160°C fan-forced. Grease shallow 2-litre (8-cup) ovenproof dish.
2 Stir milk, cream, cinnamon, vanilla bean and honey in medium saucepan until hot; strain into large heatproof jug.
3 Whisk eggs in large bowl; whisking constantly, pour hot milk mixture into egg mixture.
4 Cut each brioche into six slices and each fig into five slices. Layer brioche and figs, overlapping slightly, in dish. Pour hot milk mixture over brioche and figs; sprinkle with sugar.
5 Place pudding dish in large baking dish; pour in enough boiling water to come halfway up sides of dish.
6 Bake pudding about 40 minutes or until set. Remove pudding dish from baking dish; stand 5 minutes before serving.

prep + cook time 1 hour 15 minutes **serves** 6
tips Remove pudding from water bath immediately after cooking to prevent it from overcooking. If you can't find demerara sugar, use white sugar instead.

quince sponge pudding

4 medium quinces (1.25kg)
3 cups (750ml) water
1½ cups (330g) caster sugar
4 whole cloves
1 cinnamon stick
2 star anise
2 tablespoons icing sugar
¼ teaspoon ground cinnamon
sponge topping
3 eggs
½ cup (110g) caster sugar
¼ cup (35g) plain flour
¼ cup (35g) self-raising flour
¼ cup (35g) cornflour

1 Preheat oven to 200°C/180°C fan-forced.
2 Peel, core and slice quinces; place in shallow 2.5-litre (10-cup) ovenproof dish.
3 Stir the water, sugar, cloves, cinnamon and star anise in medium saucepan over heat, without boiling, until sugar is dissolved. Simmer, uncovered, without stirring, 2 minutes. Pour syrup over quince.
4 Bake quince, covered, about 2 hours or until quince is tender and pink. Carefully drain 2 cups (500ml) of hot liquid from quince; discard.
5 Make sponge topping; spread topping over hot quince.
6 Bake pudding about 30 minutes or until browned. Dust with sifted icing sugar and cinnamon, serve with cream and ice-cream, if you like.
sponge topping Beat eggs with electric mixer until thick and creamy. Gradually add sugar, beating until dissolved after each addition. Fold in sifted flours.

prep + cook time 2 hours 30 minutes **serves** 8

black forest upside down puddings

425g can pitted black cherries
1 tablespoon cornflour
75g dark eating chocolate,
   chopped coarsely
¼ cup (60ml) boiling water
125g butter
1 cup (220g) caster sugar
2 eggs, separated
1¼ cups (185g) plain flour
½ teaspoon bicarbonate soda
½ cup (125ml) buttermilk

custard sauce
1 tablespoon cornflour
2 cups (500ml) milk
2 tablespoons caster sugar
1 teaspoon vanilla extract
2 eggs, beaten lightly

1 Preheat oven to 180°C/160°C fan-forced. Grease six 1-cup (250ml) moulds; line bases with baking paper.
2 Drain cherries; reserve ½ cup (125ml) syrup. Blend cornflour with 2 tablespoons of the reserved syrup in small saucepan; stir in remaining syrup over high heat until mixture boils and thickens. Remove from heat; cool to room temperature. Spread mixture into moulds; top with cherries.
3 Stir chocolate and the water in medium bowl until chocolate is melted; cool to room temperature.
4 Beat butter, sugar and egg yolks in small bowl with electric mixer until light and fluffy. Transfer mixture to large bowl; stir in chocolate mixture, then sifted flour, soda and buttermilk, in two batches.
5 Beat egg whites in small bowl with electric mixer until soft peaks form; fold into chocolate mixture. Spoon mixture into moulds; cover with greased rounds of baking paper, then foil, secure with string. Place moulds in baking dish, pour in enough boiling water to come halfway up the sides of moulds.
6 Bake about 45 minutes or until firm.
7 Meanwhile, make custard sauce.
8 Turn puddings onto serving plates, serve warm with sauce.
custard sauce Blend cornflour and 2 tablespoons of the milk in small saucepan; stir in remaining milk, over high heat, until mixture boils and thickens. Remove from heat; stand 10 minutes. Whisk in sugar and extract, then egg.

prep + cook time 1 hour 15 minutes **serves** 6

cumquat jam pudding with custard cream

350g cumquats
2 cups (500ml) water
1 cup (220g) caster sugar
cake mixture
125g butter
1 teaspoon vanilla extract
½ cup (110g) caster sugar
2 eggs
2 cups (300g) self-raising flour
½ cup (125ml) milk

custard cream
¾ cups (180ml) cream
¾ cup (180ml) milk
4 egg yolks
¼ cup (55g) caster sugar
2 tablespoons orange-flavoured
   liqueur

1 Preheat oven to 180°C/160°C fan-forced. Grease six 1-cup (250ml) ovenproof dishes.

2 Cut cumquats into quarters lengthways; discard seeds. Place cumquats and the water in medium saucepan; simmer, uncovered, stirring occasionally, about 1 hour until cumquats are tender.

3 Add sugar to pan, stir over heat, without boiling, until sugar is dissolved. Simmer, uncovered, without stirring about 10 minutes or until mixture is the consistency of a soft jam.

4 Meanwhile, make cake mixture.

5 Divide cumquat mixture among dishes; top with cake mixture. Cover each dish with greased foil; secure with string. Place dishes in baking dish, pour in enough boiling water to come halfway up sides.

6 Bake puddings 30 minutes.

7 Meanwhile, make custard cream.

8 Turn puddings onto serving plates, serve with custard cream.

cake mixture Beat butter, extract and sugar in small bowl with electric mixer until thick and creamy. Beat in eggs one at a time. Transfer mixture to medium bowl; stir in sifted flour and milk, in two batches.

custard cream Bring cream and milk to the boil in medium saucepan. Whisk egg yolks and sugar in medium bowl until thick and creamy, gradually whisk into hot milk mixture. Stir over heat, without boiling, until mixture thickens slightly; stir in liqueur.

prep + cook time 1 hour 50 minutes **serves** 6

sago plum puddings with orange cream

2 cups (500ml) water
⅔ cup (130g) sago
1 teaspoon bicarbonate of soda
250g butter, softened
2 teaspoons vanilla extract
1 cup (220g) caster sugar
1 egg
½ cup (75g) plain flour
½ teaspoon bicarbonate of soda, extra
2 cups (140g) stale breadcrumbs
2 cups (320g) sultanas

orange cream
2 teaspoons finely grated orange rind
1 tablespoon orange-flavoured liqueur
1 tablespoon icing sugar
300ml thickened cream

1 Combine the water, sago and soda in medium bowl. Cover; stand overnight.

2 Preheat oven to 180°C/160°C fan-forced. Grease eight ¾-cup (180ml) ovenproof moulds.

3 Beat butter, extract, sugar and egg in small bowl with electric mixer until light and fluffy. Stir in combined sifted flour and extra soda, sago mixture, breadcrumbs and sultanas.

4 Divide mixture among moulds; cover tightly with foil. Place moulds in baking dish; pour enough boiling water into baking dish to come halfway up sides of moulds.

5 Bake puddings 3 hours, topping up water level with boiling water during cooking.

6 Meanwhile, make orange cream.

7 Turn puddings into serving bowls; serve dolloped with orange cream.

orange cream Beat ingredients in small bowl with electric mixer until soft peaks form.

prep + cook time 3 hours 10 minutes (+ standing) **serves** 8
tip Sago, also known as seed or pearl tapioca, comes from the sago palm and is used in soups and desserts, and as a thickening agent.

rhubarb and pear sponge pudding

825g can pear slices in natural juice
800g rhubarb, trimmed, cut into 4cm pieces
2 tablespoons caster sugar
2 eggs
⅓ cup (75g) caster sugar, extra
2 tablespoons plain flour
2 tablespoons self-raising flour
2 tablespoons cornflour

1 Preheat oven to 180°C/160°C fan-forced.
2 Drain pears; reserve ¾ cup (180ml) of the juice.
3 Place reserved juice, rhubarb and sugar in large saucepan; cook, stirring occasionally, about 5 minutes or until rhubarb is just tender. Stir in pears. Pour mixture into deep 1.75-litre (7-cup) ovenproof dish.
4 Meanwhile, beat eggs in small bowl with electric mixer until thick and creamy. Gradually add extra sugar, 1 tablespoon at a time, beating until sugar dissolves between additions. Gently fold in combined sifted flours.
5 Spread sponge mixture over hot rhubarb mixture. Bake pudding about 45 minutes or until browned lightly and cooked through.

prep + cook time 1 hour 10 minutes **serves** 6

rhubarb and strawberry sponge pudding

5 cups (700g) coarsely chopped, trimmed rhubarb
2 tablespoons sugar
2 tablespoons orange juice
500g strawberries, hulled, sliced thinly
sponge cake
2 eggs
½ cup (110g) caster sugar
½ cup (75g) self-raising flour
½ tablespoon cornflour

1 Preheat oven to 180°C/160°C fan-forced.
2 Cook rhubarb, sugar and juice in large saucepan over low heat, stirring, until sugar is dissolved. Cook, uncovered, further 10 minutes or until rhubarb is tender. Stir in strawberries.
3 Meanwhile, make sponge cake.
4 Divide fruit mixture among eight 1-cup (250ml) ovenproof dishes; bake 5 minutes or until fruit mixture is bubbling hot.
5 Top hot rhubarb mixture evenly with sponge cake mixture; bake about 30 minutes. Serve immediately with custard or cream.
sponge cake Beat eggs in small bowl with electric mixer about 10 minutes or until thick and creamy. Gradually add sugar, beating until dissolved between additions. Triple-sift flours; fold into egg mixture.

prep + cook time 1 hour **serves** 8
tip You will need about 10 stems of rhubarb to make this recipe.

banana pudding with espresso syrup

2 eggs
1 cup (200g) firmly packed brown sugar
2 cups mashed banana
½ cup (140g) low-fat yogurt
40g butter, melted
2 teaspoons vanilla extract
2 cups (300g) self-raising flour
1½ teaspoons ground cinnamon
1 teaspoon bicarbonate of soda
espresso syrup
¾ cup (165g) sugar
¾ cup (180ml) water
1 tablespoon instant coffee granules

1 Preheat oven to 180°C/160°C fan-forced. Grease deep 20cm-round cake pan; line base with baking paper.
2 Beat eggs in small bowl with electric mixer until thick and creamy. Add sugar; continue beating 5 minutes.
3 Fold in banana, yogurt, butter and extract, then sifted flour, cinnamon and soda; pour mixture into pan.
4 Bake pudding about 50 minutes. Stand cake in pan 5 minutes; turn onto wire rack over tray, remove paper.
5 Meanwhile, make espresso syrup.
6 Drizzle half of the hot syrup over hot cake; serve immediately with remaining hot syrup in heatproof jug and ice-cream.
espresso syrup Stir ingredients in small saucepan over heat, without boiling, until sugar is dissolved. Bring to the boil; transfer to heatproof jug.

prep + cook time 1 hour 10 minutes **serves** 8
tip You will need 4 large overripe bananas (920g) for this recipe.

apple and fig bread pudding

2 tablespoons honey
2 tablespoons water
8 slices white bread
1 medium apple (150g), cored, quartered, sliced thinly
12 dried figs (200g), halved
2 cups (500ml) skim milk
2 eggs
2 tablespoons caster sugar
½ teaspoon ground cinnamon
2 teaspoons icing sugar

1 Preheat oven to 160°C/140°C fan-forced. Grease shallow rectangular 1.25-litre (5-cup) ovenproof dish
2 Stir honey and the water in small saucepan over low heat until honey melts.
3 Cut crusts from bread; discard crusts. Halve slices diagonally; brush both sides of bread with honey mixture. Layer bread, apple and fig, overlapping pieces slightly, in dish.
4 Whisk milk, eggs and sugar together in medium bowl; strain into large jug, skimming and discarding any foam. Pour half the milk mixture over the bread; stand 5 minutes. Pour over remaining milk mixture; sprinkle with cinnamon. Place dish in large baking dish; add enough boiling water to come halfway up sides of dish.
5 Bake pudding about 45 minutes or until top is browned lightly and pudding is set. Dust with sifted icing sugar and serve with yogurt and fresh raspberries, if you like.

prep + cook time 1 hour 10 minutes **serves** 4
tips Granny smith and golden delicious are the best apple varieties to use for this recipe. Remove pudding from water bath immediately after cooking to prevent it from overcooking and becoming tough.

banana caramel puddings

90g butter, melted
½ cup (60g) ground almonds
3 egg whites
¾ cup (120g) icing sugar
¼ cup (75g) plain flour
50g butter, melted, extra
⅓ cup (75g) firmly packed brown sugar
2 medium bananas (400g), sliced thickly

1 Preheat oven to 200°C/180°C fan-forced. Grease four deep-sided 9.5cm ovenproof dishes; place on oven tray.
2 Combine butter, ground almonds, egg whites, icing sugar and flour in medium bowl until just mixed together.
3 Divide extra butter among dishes; sprinkle evenly with brown sugar. Divide banana slices then pudding mixture equally among dishes.
4 Bake puddings about 15 minutes or until browned lightly. Stand puddings in dishes 2 minutes before turning onto serving plates. Serve with ice-cream.

prep + cook time 30 minutes **serves** 4

berry coconut and yogurt parfaits

1 cup (150g) frozen mixed berries
1 tablespoon caster sugar
1 tablespoon coconut-flavoured liqueur
1 cup (250ml) raspberry and cranberry juice
12 sponge finger biscuits (140g)
500g vanilla yogurt
2 tablespoons flaked coconut, toasted

1 Blend or process berries, sugar, liqueur and ¼ cup (60ml) of the juice until smooth.
2 Dip biscuits in remaining juice; divide among six 1½-cup (375ml) serving glasses.
3 Divide half the yogurt among glasses; top with half the berry mixture. Repeat layering with remaining yogurt and berry mixture. Sprinkle with coconut.

prep time 10 minutes **serves** 6
tips You do not need to defrost the berries before blending. This dessert can be made several hours ahead; store, covered, in the refrigerator.

lemon curd, blueberry and meringue trifle

2 cups (500ml) grape juice
85g packet blueberry jelly crystals
200g sponge cake, cut into 3cm pieces
¼ cup (60ml) sweet sherry
2 teaspoons finely grated lemon rind
¾ cup (180ml) lemon juice
1 cup (220g) caster sugar
4 eggs
80g butter, chopped coarsely
1 teaspoon gelatine
1 tablespoon water
300ml thickened cream
50g meringue, chopped coarsely
2 cups (300g) fresh blueberries

1 Bring grape juice to the boil in small saucepan; stir in jelly crystals until dissolved. Pour jelly mixture into shallow container. Refrigerate about 20 minutes or until jelly is almost set.
2 Place cake in 3-litre (12-cup) bowl; sprinkle with sherry.
3 Combine rind, juice, sugar, eggs and butter in medium heatproof bowl. Place over medium saucepan of simmering water; cook, stirring, about 15 minutes or until curd coats the back of a spoon.
4 Sprinkle gelatine over the water in small heatproof jug. Stand jug in small saucepan of simmering water; stir until gelatine dissolves. Stir gelatine mixture into warm lemon curd. Cool to room temperature.
5 Pour jelly over cake; refrigerate 15 minutes. Top with lemon curd. Cover; refrigerate 3 hours or overnight.
6 Just before serving, beat cream in small bowl with electric mixer until soft peaks form; spread over curd. Sprinkle with meringue and berries.

prep + cook time 40 minutes (+ refrigeration and cooling) **serves** 6

classic trifle

85g packet raspberry jelly crystals
250g sponge cake, cut into 3cm pieces
¼ cup (60ml) sweet sherry
¼ cup (30g) custard powder
¼ cup (55g) caster sugar
½ teaspoon vanilla extract
1½ cups (375ml) milk
825g can sliced peaches, drained
300ml thickened cream
2 tablespoons flaked almonds, roasted

1 Make jelly according to directions on packet; pour into shallow container.
Refrigerate 20 minutes or until jelly is almost set.
2 Arrange cake in 3-litre (12-cup) bowl; sprinkle with sherry.
3 Blend custard powder, sugar and extract with a little of the milk in
small saucepan; stir in remaining milk. Stir over heat until mixture boils
and thickens. Cover surface with plastic wrap; cool.
4 Pour jelly over cake; refrigerate 15 minutes. Top with peaches.
Stir a third of the cream into custard; pour over peaches.
5 Whip remaining cream; spread over custard, sprinkle with nuts.
Refrigerate 3 hours or overnight.

prep + cook time 40 minutes (+ refrigeration) **serves** 8

chocolate and berry trifle

150g dark eating chocolate, chopped coarsely
¾ cup (180ml) thickened cream
1 egg, separated
2 teaspoons caster sugar
85g packet cherry jelly crystals
325g plain chocolate cake, chopped coarsely
300g fresh mixed berries

1 Stir chocolate and cream in small saucepan over low heat until smooth. Remove from heat; transfer to medium bowl, stir in egg yolk.
2 Beat egg white and sugar in small bowl with electric mixer until sugar dissolves; fold into chocolate mixture. Refrigerate mousse 3 hours or overnight.
3 Make jelly according to directions on packet; pour into shallow container. Refrigerate 20 minutes or until jelly is almost set.
4 Place cake pieces in six 1-cup (250ml) serving glasses. Pour jelly over cake; refrigerate 15 minutes.
5 Divide half the berries over the jelly; top with scoops of mousse, then remaining berries.

prep + cook time 40 minutes (+ refrigeration) **serves** 6

tropical fruit trifle

85g packet mango jelly crystals
¼ cup (30g) custard powder
⅓ cup (75g) caster sugar
½ teaspoon vanilla extract
1½ cups (375ml) milk
⅓ cup (80ml) pineapple juice
⅓ cup (80ml) coconut-flavoured liqueur
6 sponge finger biscuits (70g)
⅔ cup (160ml) thickened cream
125g cream cheese, softened
1 medium kiwifruit (85g), sliced
1 medium mango (430g), sliced
1 medium star fruit (160g), sliced
2 tablespoons passionfruit pulp

1 Make jelly according to directions on packet; pour into shallow container. Refrigerate 20 minutes or until jelly is almost set.
2 Blend custard powder, half the sugar, and extract with a little of the milk in small saucepan; stir in remaining milk. Stir over heat until mixture boils and thickens. Cover custard surface with plastic wrap; cool.
3 Combine juice and liqueur in small bowl. Soak sponge fingers, one at a time, in juice mixture; place over base of shallow 2-litre (8-cup) serving dish. Pour jelly over sponge fingers, cover; refrigerate 15 minutes or until jelly is set.
4 Stir half the cream into custard; pour over jelly.
5 Beat cream cheese with remaining cream and sugar in small bowl with electric mixer until smooth. Spread over custard, top with fruit and pulp. Refrigerate 3 hours or overnight.

prep + cook time 30 minutes (+ refrigeration) **serves** 6

raspberry and chocolate mousse trifle

150g dark eating chocolate, chopped coarsely
½ cup (125ml) thickened cream
1 egg, separated
2 teaspoons caster sugar
85g packet raspberry jelly crystals
200g packaged chocolate sponge finger cakes (about 6)
¼ cup (60ml) coffee-flavoured liqueur
1 cup (135g) raspberries
300ml thickened cream, extra

1 Stir chocolate and cream in small saucepan over heat, without boiling, until smooth. Remove from heat; whisk in egg yolk. Transfer mixture to medium bowl.
2 Beat egg white and sugar in small bowl with electric mixer until sugar is dissolved. Gently fold egg white mixture into chocolate mixture. Cover; refrigerate mousse 3 hours or overnight.
3 Meanwhile, make jelly according to manufacturer's instructions; refrigerate until jelly is set to the consistency of unbeaten egg white.
4 Cut sponge fingers into 1.5cm slices. Place slices over base and around side of deep 2-litre (8-cup) large serving bowl; drizzle evenly with liqueur. Pour jelly over sponge fingers; refrigerate until jelly sets.
5 Sprinkle half of the raspberries over jelly; spread evenly with mousse. Top with whipped extra cream and remaining raspberries. Sprinkle with chocolate shavings, if you like.

prep + cook time 30 minutes (+ refrigeration) **serves** 6
tips Small sponge finger cakes filled with mock cream are available in 200g packages at most supermarkets. Mousse can be prepared up to two days ahead; trifle can be assembled a day ahead. If fresh raspberries are not available, frozen raspberries, thawed, can be substituted.

peach and raspberry trifle

85g packet raspberry jelly crystals
250g unfilled packaged sponge cake
2 tablespoons raspberry jam
½ cup (125ml) sweet sherry
¼ cup (30g) custard powder
¼ cup (55g) caster sugar
1½ cups (375ml) milk
½ teaspoon vanilla extract
300ml thickened cream
825g can sliced peaches, drained
2 tablespoons flaked almonds, roasted

1 Make jelly according to manufacturer's instructions; refrigerate until jelly is set to the consistency of unbeaten egg white.
2 Meanwhile, split cake in half horizontally through centre; sandwich cake halves with jam. Cut cake into 3cm squares.
3 Place cake in 2.5-litre (10-cup) deep serving bowl; sprinkle with sherry.
4 Combine custard powder and sugar in medium saucepan. Gradually blend in milk; stir over heat until mixture boils and thickens. Remove from heat, stir in extract and ½ cup of the cream. Cover surface with plastic wrap; cool to room temperature.
5 Meanwhile, pour jelly over cake, cover; refrigerate until jelly sets.
6 Top jelly with peaches, then with custard.
7 Beat remaining cream in small bowl with electric mixer until soft peaks form. Spread cream over custard; refrigerate 2 hours or overnight. Sprinkle with nuts just before serving.

prep + cook time 40 minutes (+ refrigeration) **serves** 10

mango and lemon chiffon trifle

200g unfilled packaged sponge cake
85g packet mango jelly crystals
1 large mango (600g), sliced thinly
lemon chiffon
2 eggs, separated
2 egg yolks
½ cup (110g) caster sugar
1 teaspoon finely grated lemon rind
1 teaspoon gelatine
¼ cup (60ml) water
1 tablespoon lemon juice
¾ cup (180ml) thickened cream, whipped

1 Cut sponge into 1cm squares; divide among six 2-cup (500ml) serving glasses.
2 Make jelly according to directions on packet. Pour half of the warm jelly mixture over sponge, cover; refrigerate until set. Cover remaining jelly, refrigerate until the consistency of unbeaten egg white.
3 Meanwhile, make lemon chiffon.
4 Reserve six slices of the mango. Blend or process remaining mango until smooth. Spoon soft jelly over sponge; top with mango puree. Spoon lemon chiffon over puree; refrigerate until set. Top each trifle with one reserved mango slice.
lemon chiffon Beat all egg yolks, half of the sugar and the rind in small bowl with electric mixer until thick and creamy. Sprinkle gelatine over the water in small heatproof jug; stand jug in small saucepan of simmering water. Stir until gelatine dissolves; add juice, stir into egg mixture. Transfer to large bowl. Beat egg whites in small bowl with electric mixer until soft peaks form. Gradually add remaining sugar, 1 tablespoon at a time, beating until sugar dissolves between additions; fold into lemon mixture, then fold in cream.

prep + cook time 35 minutes (+ refrigeration) **serves** 6

summer berry clafoutis

200g boysenberries
200g blackberries
150g raspberries
100g blueberries
3 eggs
⅓ cup (75g) caster sugar
1 teaspoon vanilla extract
⅓ cup (50g) plain flour
1 tablespoon self-raising flour
¾ cup (180ml) milk

1 Preheat oven to 180°C/160°C fan-forced. Grease six 1-cup (250ml) shallow ovenproof dishes; place on oven tray.
2 Divide berries among dishes. Whisk eggs, sugar and extract in medium bowl until frothy. Whisk in sifted flours and milk until just combined. Pour mixture, over the back of a spoon, into dishes.
3 Bake clafoutis about 35 minutes or until set. Serve warm, dusted with sifted icing sugar and cream, if you like.

prep + cook time 50 minutes **serves** 6
tip While we used the best of the season here, any combination of berries would be delicious.

pear charlottes with fig syrup

5 large pears (1.8kg)
1 cup (220g) firmly packed brown sugar
1 cinnamon stick
1 cup (250ml) water
16 slices day-old white bread
90g butter, melted
4 dried figs, sliced thinly
¼ cup (60ml) brandy

1 Preheat oven to 200°C/180°C fan-forced. Grease four 1-cup (250ml) ovenproof dishes.
2 Peel and core pears; chop coarsely. Place pear in medium saucepan with sugar, cinnamon and the water; bring to the boil. Reduce heat; simmer, uncovered, about 10 minutes or until pears are tender. Strain pears over medium bowl; reserve syrup and cinnamon.
3 Cut eight 8.5cm rounds from eight bread slices. Remove crusts from remaining bread slices; cut each slice into three 3cm-wide strips. Halve each strip crossways.
4 Combine butter and 2 tablespoons of the syrup in small bowl; brush butter mixture on one side of all bread pieces. Place one bread round, buttered-side down, in each dish; line side of each dish with bread fingers, buttered-side against dish, overlapping slightly. Fill centres with pear; top with remaining bread rounds, buttered-side up.
5 Bake charlottes about 30 minutes or until browned lightly.
6 Meanwhile, bring 1 cup of the reserved syrup and cinnamon to the boil in small saucepan; add figs. Reduce heat; simmer, uncovered, about 5 minutes or until syrup reduces by half. Add brandy; simmer, uncovered, 3 minutes.
7 Turn charlottes onto serving plates; spoon fig syrup over each charlotte.

prep + cook time 1 hour **serves** 4
tip You can replace pears with apples or quinces, if you prefer.

apple charlotte

6 medium apples (900g), peeled,
  cored, chopped coarsely
1 teaspoon grated lemon rind
1 tablespoon lemon juice
½ teaspoon ground cinnamon
¼ teaspoon ground nutmeg
¼ cup (55g) caster sugar
¼ cup (60ml) water
13 slices white bread
100g unsalted butter, melted
¼ cup (80ml) apricot jam
2 tablespoons water, extra

quick cinnamon custard
¼ teaspoon ground cinnamon
¾ cup (180ml) pouring custard
2 tablespoons milk

1 Combine apples, rind, juice, cinnamon, nutmeg, sugar and the water in large saucepan; simmer, stirring occasionally, about 10 minutes or until apples are tender. Cool; strain.
2 Remove crusts from bread slices. Cut two 5.5cm rounds from each of two slices; cut remaining 11 slices into three strips each.
3 Preheat oven to 200°C/180°C fan-forced. Grease four 1-cup (250ml) ovenproof moulds.
4 Brush both sides of bread with butter, place rounds in base of each mould. Line sides of moulds with bread strips, slightly overlapping edges, extending bread 1.5cm above top edge of mould.
5 Pack apple mixture firmly into moulds. Fold bread toward centre to cover filling, press firmly to seal. Place moulds on oven tray.
6 Bake charlottes about 35 minutes or until bread is golden brown. Stand in moulds 10 minutes before turning onto serving plates.
7 Meanwhile, make quick cinnamon custard.
8 Simmer jam and extra water in small saucepan, stirring occasionally, about 5 minutes or until thickened slightly; strain. Brush glaze over charlottes. Serve charlottes warm with custard.
quick cinnamon custard Combine ingredients in small jug.

prep + cook time 1 hour **serves** 4
tip We used metal charlotte moulds, but soufflé dishes can also be used.

chocolate cherry meringue desserts

250g chocolate cake, chopped
½ cup (110g) sugar
½ cup (125ml) water
¼ cup (60ml) amaretto
425g canned cherries, drained
3 egg yolks
2 teaspoons cornflour
¼ cup (55g) sugar, extra
1½ cups (375ml) milk
125g cream cheese, chopped
meringue
3 egg whites
½ cup (110g) caster sugar

1 Divide cake into six 1-cup (250ml) ovenproof dishes.
2 Stir sugar and the water in saucepan constantly, over heat, without boiling, until sugar is dissolved. Bring to the boil; boil, uncovered, 2 minutes, without stirring. Remove from heat; stir in liqueur, pour over cake. Divide cherries evenly over cake.
3 Preheat oven to 160°C/140°C fan-forced.
4 Meanwhile, combine egg yolks, cornflour and extra sugar in medium saucepan; gradually stir in milk, over heat, stirring constantly, until custard boils and thickens. Reduce heat; stir in cream cheese until melted. Remove from heat. Divide custard evenly into dishes; stand 15 minutes.
5 Make meringue; spread over custard.
6 Bake desserts about 12 minutes. Increase oven temperature to 180°C/160°C fan-forced; bake further 5 minutes or until meringue is lightly browned.
meringue Beat egg whites is small bowl with electric mixer until soft peaks form; gradually add sugar, beat until dissolved.

prep + cook time 45 minutes   **serves** 6
tips Amaretto is an almond-flavoured liqueur. If you prefer a tart flavour, use bottled morello cherries. Desserts can be layered in dishes several hours ahead; top with meringue just before serving.

lime coconut bake

1 tablespoon chopped glacé ginger
2 tablespoons chopped roasted unsalted macadamias
½ cup (110g) firmly packed brown sugar
¼ cup (90g) golden syrup
¼ cup (60ml) lime juice
4 eggs, beaten lightly
400ml can coconut cream
2 teaspoons grated lime rind
¼ teaspoon ground ginger
½ teaspoon ground cinnamon

1 Preheat oven to 180°C/160°C fan-forced. Grease six ¾-cup (180ml) ovenproof moulds. Sprinkle base of moulds with combined glacé ginger and nuts.
2 Stir sugar, golden syrup and juice in small saucepan, over heat, without boiling, until sugar is dissolved; cool to room temperature.
3 Combine egg and coconut cream in medium bowl; stir in rind, ground ginger and cinnamon. Stir syrup into egg mixture; pour mixture into moulds.
4 Place moulds in baking dish, then pour in enough boiling water to come halfway up the sides of moulds.
5 Bake about 1 hour or until just set. Remove moulds from water; cool, refrigerate overnight. Serve either hot or cold with whipped cream and toasted shredded coconut.

prep + cook time 1 hour 30 minutes (+ refrigeration) **serves** 6

creamy lemon crumble

1 tablespoon cornflour
½ cup (110g) caster sugar
2 teaspoons grated lemon rind
½ cup (125ml) lemon juice
2 tablespoons water
3 eggs, beaten lightly
15g butter
⅓ cup (80g) sour cream
crumble topping
½ cup (75g) plain flour
1 cup (90g) rolled oats
125g butter
2 tablespoons caster sugar
¼ cup (20g) shredded coconut
½ cup (70g) slivered almonds
¼ cup (40g) dried currants

1 Preheat oven to 200°C/180°C fan-forced. Grease six ½-cup (125ml) ovenproof dishes.
2 Stir cornflour and sugar with rind, juice and the water in medium heatproof bowl over medium saucepan of simmering water; stir in eggs and butter until mixture is thickened. Remove from heat; stir in sour cream. Pour custard into dishes.
3 Make crumble topping; sprinkle topping over custard.
4 Bake crumble about 20 minutes or until topping is crisp.
crumble topping Sift flour into medium bowl, stir in oats, rub in butter. Stir in remaining ingredients.

prep + cook time 35 minutes **serves** 6

mocha pear crumble

2 medium pears (460g), peeled, cored, chopped finely
25g dark eating chocolate, chopped coarsely
mocha crumble
1 teaspoon instant coffee granules
½ teaspoon hot water
¼ cup (35g) plain flour
1 tablespoon self-raising flour
2 tablespoons raw sugar
35g unsalted butter, chopped
2 teaspoons cocoa powder

1 Make mocha crumble.
2 Preheat oven to 200°C/180°C fan-forced. Grease six ⅓-cup (80ml) ovenproof dishes; place on oven tray.
3 Divide pear and chocolate among dishes; coarsely grate crumble dough over pear mixture.
4 Bake crumble about 20 minutes. Stand 5 minutes before serving with cream or ice-cream.
mocha crumble Dissolve coffee in the water in processor. Add remaining ingredients; process until combined. Wrap dough in plastic wrap; freeze about 1 hour or until firm.

prep + cook time 35 minutes (+ refrigeration) **serves** 6

plum cobbler

825g can plums in syrup
¾ cup (110g) self-raising flour
¼ cup (55g) caster sugar
1 teaspoon ground cinnamon
60g butter, chopped
1 egg yolk
¼ cup (60ml) buttermilk, approximately
2 tablespoons coarsely chopped roasted hazelnuts
2 tablespoons icing sugar

1 Preheat oven to 180°C/160°C fan-forced.
2 Drain plums over medium saucepan. Halve plums; discard stones. Add plums to pan; bring to the boil. Reduce heat; simmer, uncovered, about 5 minutes or until plums soften.
3 Strain plums; reserve ½ cup liquid. Place plums and reserved liquid in 1-litre (4-cup) ovenproof dish; place dish on oven tray.
4 Sift flour, caster sugar and cinnamon into medium bowl; rub in butter. Stir in egg yolk and enough of the buttermilk to make a soft, sticky dough. Drop heaped teaspoons of the mixture over hot plums; sprinkle with nuts.
5 Bake cobbler about 30 minutes or until browned lightly. Serve dusted with sifted icing sugar and cream or ice-cream.

prep + cook time 45 minutes **serves** 4

blueberry crumble

¼ cup (55g) brown sugar
¼ cup (55g) caster sugar
¾ cup (110g) plain flour
1 teaspoon ground cinnamon
100g butter, chopped coarsely
¾ cup (65g) rolled oats
½ cup (70g) coarsely chopped roasted macadamias
500g blueberries
1 tablespoon lemon juice
¼ cup (55g) caster sugar, extra

1 Preheat oven to 200°C/180°C fan-forced.
2 Sift sugars, flour and cinnamon into medium bowl; rub in butter.
Stir in oats and nuts.
3 Combine blueberries with juice and extra sugar in medium bowl.
4 Divide blueberry mixture among four 1-cup (250ml) ovenproof dishes;
sprinkle with crumble topping.
5 Bake crumbles about 40 minutes. Serve with vanilla ice-cream.

prep + cook time 50 minutes **serves** 4
tip You can use fresh or frozen blueberries for this recipe, or a
combination of both.

apple and pear crumble

3 medium apples (450g)
3 medium pears (690g)
¼ cup (55g) caster sugar
¼ cup (60ml) water
crumble topping
½ cup (60g) ground almonds
⅓ cup (60g) rice flour
⅓ cup (75g) firmly packed brown sugar
60g butter, chopped
1 teaspoon ground cinnamon

1 Preheat oven to 180°C/160°C fan-forced. Grease deep 1.5-litre (6-cup) ovenproof dish.
2 Peel, core and quarter apples and pears; slice fruit thickly. Place fruit, sugar and the water in large saucepan; cook, covered, about 10 minutes or until fruit is just tender. Drain; discard liquid.
3 Meanwhile, make crumble topping.
4 Place apple mixture in dish; sprinkle with topping. Bake crumble about 25 minutes.
crumble topping Blend or process ingredients until combined.

variations
muesli crumble Prepare half the amount of basic crumble topping; stir in 1 cup (100g) toasted muesli.
coconut crumble Prepare half the amount of basic crumble topping; stir in ½ cup (40g) shredded coconut.

prep + cook time 45 minutes **serves** 4
tip This recipe is gluten-free, wheat-free, yeast-free and egg-free.

glacé fruit puddings with ginger syrup

100g butter, softened
1 teaspoon finely grated lemon rind
¾ cup (165g) caster sugar
2 eggs
½ cup (75g) plain flour
½ cup (75g) self-raising flour
½ cup (60g) ground almonds
⅓ cup (80ml) milk
4 slices (110g) glacé pineapple, chopped finely
⅓ cup (85g) finely chopped glacé apricots
⅓ cup (85g) finely chopped glacé figs
ginger syrup
½ cup (125ml) water
½ cup (110g) caster sugar
2cm piece fresh ginger (10g), grated

1 Preheat oven to 180°C/160°C fan-forced. Grease six ¾-cup (180ml) pudding moulds or ovenproof tea cups; place on oven tray.
2 Beat butter, rind and sugar in small bowl with electric mixer until light and fluffy. Beat in eggs, one at a time.
3 Transfer mixture to medium bowl; stir in sifted flours, ground almonds, milk and fruit. Spread mixture into moulds; bake about 35 minutes.
4 Meanwhile, make ginger syrup.
5 Remove puddings from oven; pour hot syrup over hot puddings in moulds. Stand 5 minutes before turning onto serving plates (or serve in tea cups). Serve warm.
ginger syrup Combine ingredients in small saucepan; stir over low heat, without boiling, until sugar dissolves. Bring to the boil, reduce heat, simmer, uncovered, without stirring, about 3 minutes or until syrup thickens slightly.

prep + cook time 50 minutes **serves** 6
tip Puddings are best made just before serving. The mixture may curdle when the second egg is added, however, it will become smooth again once the flour is stirred in.

berry and hazelnut crumble

2 cups (300g) frozen mixed berries
1 tablespoon lemon juice
2 tablespoons brown sugar
½ cup (60g) finely chopped roasted hazelnuts
2 tablespoons plain flour
20g cold butter
¼ cup (20g) rolled oats

1 Preheat oven to 220°C/200°C fan-forced. Grease four shallow
¾-cup (180ml) ovenproof dishes; place on oven tray.
2 Combine berries, juice, half the sugar and half the nuts in medium
bowl; divide mixture among dishes.
3 Blend or process remaining sugar and nuts with flour and butter until
ingredients come together; stir in oats. Sprinkle over berry mixture.
4 Bake crumbles about 20 minutes or until browned lightly.

prep + cook time 30 minutes **serves** 4

pineapple crunch

850g can crushed pineapple, drained
2 small nashis (360g), chopped coarsely
1 tablespoon Malibu liqueur
3 cups (150g) cornflakes
2 tablespoons pepitas
2 tablespoons sunflower seeds
⅓ cup (95g) low-fat yogurt
2 tablespoons honey

1 Preheat oven to 180°C/160°C fan-forced. Grease four 1-cup (250ml) ovenproof dishes; place on oven tray.
2 Combine pineapple, nashi and liqueur in medium bowl; divide mixture among dishes.
3 Using one hand, crumble cereal in same bowl; stir in seeds, yogurt and honey. Divide mixture among dishes.
4 Bake about 20 minutes or until browned lightly. Serve topped with yogurt or ice-cream.

prep + cook time 30 minutes **serves** 4
tip You can substitute chopped, drained canned peaches or apricots for the pineapple in this recipe.

rhubarb and apple crumble

1kg trimmed stems rhubarb (about 16)
2 medium green apples (300g)
¼ cup (55g) sugar
2 tablespoons water
crumble topping
1 cup (40g) cornflakes
⅓ cup (25g) desiccated coconut
⅓ cup (75g) firmly packed brown sugar
⅓ cup (80ml) sweetened condensed milk

1 Preheat oven to 180°C/160°C fan-forced.
2 Cut rhubarb into 2.5cm lengths. Peel and core apples, cut into quarters, slice thinly. Cook rhubarb, apple, sugar and the water in medium saucepan over medium heat about 15 minutes or until tender.
3 Make crumble topping.
4 Spoon rhubarb mixture into 1-litre (4-cup) ovenproof dish or six ¾-cup (180ml) ovenproof dishes; sprinkle with topping.
5 Bake crumble 15 minutes or until topping is golden brown. Serve topped with whipped cream or with ice-cream.
crumble topping Combine ingredients in medium bowl.

prep + cook time 45 minutes **serves** 6

pear and plum amaretti crumble

825g can plums in syrup, drained, halved, stoned
825g can pear halves in natural juice, drained, halved
1 teaspoon ground cardamom
125g amaretti, crushed
1/3 cup (50g) plain flour
1/3 cup (35g) almond meal
1/2 cup (70g) slivered almonds
100g butter, chopped

1 Preheat oven to 200°C/180°C fan-forced. Grease deep 1.5-litre (6 cup) ovenproof dish.
2 Combine plums, pears and cardamom in dish.
3 Combine amaretti, flour, almond meal and nuts in medium bowl; rub in butter. Sprinkle evenly over plum mixture.
4 Bake crumble about 15 minutes or until golden brown.

prep + cook time 25 minutes **serves** 4
tip You could also make this crumble in four 1 1/2-cup (375ml) ovenproof dishes; bake 15 minutes.

peach and raspberry meringue roll

4 egg whites
¾ cup (165g) caster sugar
1 teaspoon cornflour
1 teaspoon white vinegar
⅓ cup (25g) flaked almonds
3 medium peaches (450g)
300ml thickened cream
1 tablespoon peach schnapps
120g raspberries

1 Preheat oven to 180°C/160°C fan-forced. Grease 25cm x 30cm swiss roll pan; line base and long sides with baking paper, extending paper 5cm over edges.
2 Beat egg whites in small bowl with electric mixer until soft peaks form. Gradually add sugar, 1 tablespoon at a time, beating until sugar dissolves between additions. Fold in cornflour and vinegar. Spread mixture into pan; sprinkle with almonds.
3 Bake meringue about 20 minutes or until browned lightly. Turn meringue onto baking-paper-covered wire rack; peel away lining paper. Cool.
4 Meanwhile, cut small cross in stem end of each peach; place in medium heatproof bowl. Cover with boiling water; stand 30 seconds, drain. Peel skin from peaches; slice flesh thinly.
5 Beat cream and schnapps in small bowl with electric mixer until soft peaks form; spread evenly over meringue. Top with peach and raspberries. Roll meringue firmly, from long side, by lifting paper and using it to guide roll into shape.

prep + cook time 45 minutes **serves** 8

coffee and pecan puddings
with caramel sauce

¾ cup (90g) coarsely chopped roasted pecans
300ml cream
1½ cups (330g) firmly packed brown sugar
100g cold butter, chopped
125g butter, softened
1 teaspoon vanilla extract
½ cup (110g) caster sugar
2 eggs
1 cup (150g) self-raising flour
¼ cup (35g) plain flour
¼ cup (60ml) milk
1 tablespoon finely ground espresso coffee

1 Preheat oven to 180°C/160°C fan-forced. Grease six ¾-cup (180ml) metal moulds or ovenproof dishes; line bases with baking paper.
2 Divide nuts among moulds; place moulds on oven tray.
3 Stir cream, brown sugar and chopped butter in small saucepan over heat, without boiling, until sugar dissolves. Reduce heat; simmer, uncovered, without stirring, about 5 minutes or until mixture thickens slightly. Spoon 2 tablespoons of the sauce over nuts in each mould; reserve remaining sauce.
4 Beat softened butter, extract and caster sugar in small bowl with electric mixer until light and fluffy. Beat in eggs, one at a time. Stir in sifted flours, milk and coffee; divide mixture among moulds.
5 Bake puddings 30 minutes. Stand puddings 5 minutes before turning onto serving plates. Serve puddings with warm sauce.

prep + cook time 50 minutes   **serves** 6
tip The caramel sauce and puddings can be made several hours ahead and reheated before serving.

hazelnut tiramisu

1 tablespoon instant coffee granules
2 tablespoons caster sugar
⅔ cup (160ml) boiling water
⅓ cup (80ml) hazelnut-flavoured liqueur
½ cup (125ml) cream
1 cup (250g) mascarpone cheese
12 sponge finger biscuits (140g)
¼ cup (25g) coarsely grated dark chocolate
½ cup (70g) coarsely chopped roasted hazelnuts

1 Dissolve coffee and half the sugar in the water in medium heatproof
bowl. Stir in liqueur; cool.
2 Meanwhile, beat cream and remaining sugar in small bowl with electric
mixer until soft peaks form; fold in mascarpone.
3 Dip biscuits, one at a time, in coffee mixture; place in single layer in
shallow 2-litre (8-cup) serving dish. Pour any remaining coffee mixture
over biscuits. Spread cream mixture over biscuits; sprinkle with combined
chocolate and nuts. Refrigerate until required.

prep time 20 minutes (+ refrigeration) **serves** 6

chocolate pecan pudding

200g ciabatta, sliced thickly
100g dark eating chocolate, chopped coarsely
⅓ cup (40g) coarsely chopped roasted pecans
custard
1½ cups (375ml) milk
2 cups (500ml) cream
⅓ cup (75g) caster sugar
½ teaspoon vanilla extract
4 eggs

1 Preheat oven to 160°C/140°C fan-forced.
2 Make custard.
3 Grease shallow 2-litre (8-cup) ovenproof dish. Layer bread, chocolate and nuts, overlapping slices slightly, in dish. Pour custard over bread.
4 Place dish in large baking dish; add enough boiling water to come halfway up sides of dish.
5 Bake pudding about 45 minutes or until pudding sets. Remove pudding from baking dish; stand 5 minutes before serving.
custard Combine milk, cream, sugar and extract in medium saucepan; bring to the boil. Whisk eggs in large bowl; whisking constantly, gradually add hot milk mixture to egg mixture.

prep + cook time 1 hour **serves** 6

pecan dumplings in honey syrup

1⅓ cups (200g) self-raising flour
½ teaspoon mixed spice
30g butter
½ cup (60g) coarsely chopped pecans
⅔ cup (160ml) milk, approximately
honey syrup
1 cup (220g) sugar
⅓ cup (115g) honey
2½ cups (625ml) water
30g butter

1 Make honey syrup.
2 Meanwhile, sift flour and spice into large bowl; rub in butter, stir in nuts. Make well in centre, stir in enough milk to make a soft sticky dough.
3 Knead dough gently on floured surface until smooth; divide dough into 12 pieces, knead each piece into a smooth ball.
4 Place balls into simmering honey syrup; simmer, covered about 20 minutes or until syrup is thickened and dumplings are cooked through. Serve hot dumplings sprinkled with extra chopped pecans, honey syrup and ice-cream.
honey syrup Stir ingredients in large saucepan over heat, without boiling, until sugar is dissolved; bring to the boil. Reduce heat to simmer before adding dumplings.

prep + cook time 40 minutes **serves** 6
tip Dumplings are best made close to serving time.

MILK PUDDINGS

glacé fruit and citrus frozen puddings

1½ cups (280g) finely chopped mixed glacé fruit
½ cup (170g) orange marmalade
2 tablespoons Grand Marnier
2 teaspoons finely grated orange rind
¼ cup coarsely chopped fresh mint
2 litres vanilla ice-cream, softened
bitter orange sauce
⅔ cup (160ml) orange juice
⅓ cup (115g) orange marmalade
2 tablespoons lemon juice
1 tablespoon Grand Marnier

1 Line eight 1-cup (250ml) moulds with plastic wrap.
2 Combine glacé fruit, marmalade, liqueur, rind and mint in medium bowl.
Place ice-cream in large bowl; fold in fruit mixture. Divide ice-cream
mixture among moulds; cover with foil.
3 Freeze puddings 3 hours or overnight.
4 Make bitter orange sauce.
5 Turn puddings onto serving plates; serve with bitter orange sauce.
bitter orange sauce Combine ingredients in small jug.

prep time 40 minutes (+ freezing) **serves** 8

coco-cherry ice-cream timbale

2 litres (8 cups) vanilla ice-cream
2 x 85g Cherry Ripe bars, chopped coarsely
1 cup (140g) vienna almonds, chopped coarsely
50g pink marshmallows, chopped coarsely
50g dark chocolate, chopped coarsely
pink food colouring
300ml cream
100g white chocolate, chopped finely

1 Soften ice-cream in large bowl; stir in Cherry Ripe, nuts, marshmallow, dark chocolate and enough colouring to tint the ice-cream pink. Divide mixture among eight 1-cup (250ml) moulds. Cover with foil; freeze 3 hours or overnight.
2 Bring cream to the boil in small saucepan. Remove from heat; add white chocolate, stir until chocolate melts.
3 Turn ice-cream timbales onto serving plates; drizzle with warm white chocolate sauce.

prep + cook time 25 minutes (+ freezing) **serves** 8
tips Use a good quality vanilla ice-cream. Vienna almonds are almonds coated in a toffee mixture; scorched almonds can be used instead.

white chocolate frozen christmas pudding

½ cup (75g) dried cranberries
½ cup (115g) finely chopped glacé pineapple
¼ cup (60ml) brandy
2 litres vanilla ice-cream, softened
2 cups (280g) vienna almonds, chopped coarsely
360g white eating chocolate, melted

1 Line 17.5cm, 1.75-litre (7-cup) pudding basin with plastic wrap, extending plastic 5cm over edge of basin.
2 Combine fruit and brandy in large bowl; stand 30 minutes.
3 Stir ice-cream and nuts into fruit mixture until combined. Pack ice-cream mixture into basin, cover with foil; freeze overnight.
4 Turn pudding onto tray; remove plastic wrap, return pudding to freezer.
5 Cut a piece of paper into 35cm circle to use as a guide. Cover paper with a large sheet of plastic wrap. Spread chocolate over plastic wrap. Quickly drape plastic, chocolate-side down, over pudding. Smooth pudding with hands before gently peeling away plastic wrap. Trim base; centre pudding on serving plate.

prep time 25 minutes (+ standing and freezing) **serves** 12
tips Decorate pudding with frozen cherries and dust with icing sugar just before serving, if desired. This recipe can be made 1 week ahead. Add chocolate coating up to 3 hours before serving.

frozen choc fruit cake

½ cup (95g) coarsely chopped
   dried figs
¼ cup (40g) coarsely chopped
   raisins
¼ cup (50g) coarsely chopped
   dried prunes
¼ cup (60g) coarsely chopped
   glacé cherries
4 fresh dates (100g), seeded,
   chopped coarsely
2 teaspoons finely grated
   orange rind
½ cup (125ml) brandy
125g butter
½ cup (75g) plain flour

½ cup (110g) firmly packed
   brown sugar
1 cup (250ml) milk
600ml thickened cream
⅔ cup (220g) chocolate
   hazelnut spread
1 teaspoon ground nutmeg
1 teaspoon ground cinnamon
4 egg yolks
⅓ cup (50g) roasted hazelnuts,
   chopped coarsely
200g dark eating chocolate,
   chopped finely
200g dark eating chocolate,
   melted, extra

1 Combine fruit, rind and brandy in large bowl. Cover tightly with plastic
wrap; store in a cool, dark place overnight or up to a week, stirring every day.
2 Line 17.5cm, 1.75-litre (7-cup) pudding basin with plastic wrap,
extending plastic 5cm over edge of basin.
3 Melt butter in medium saucepan, add flour; stir over heat until bubbling.
Remove from heat; stir in sugar then milk and half of the cream. Stir over
medium heat until mixture boils and thickens. Transfer to large bowl; stir
in spread, spices and yolks. Cover surface of mixture with plastic wrap;
refrigerate 1 hour.
4 Stir in fruit mixture, nuts and chopped chocolate. Beat remaining cream
in small bowl with electric mixer until soft peaks form, fold into pudding
mixture. Spoon mixture into prepared basin, tap basin lightly to remove air
bubbles. Cover with foil; freeze 3 hours or overnight.
5 Turn pudding onto tray; remove plastic wrap, return pudding to freezer.
6 Cut a 35cm circle from a piece of paper to use as a guide; cover paper
with plastic wrap. Spread melted chocolate over plastic wrap then quickly
drape plastic, chocolate-side down, over pudding. Quickly smooth with
hands, avoiding deep pleats in the plastic. Freeze until firm. Peel away
plastic; trim away excess chocolate. Serve with seasonal fruit.

prep + cook time 1 hour (+ standing, refrigeration and freezing)

bread and butter pudding

6 thin slices white bread (270g)
40g butter, softened
4 eggs
⅓ cup (75g) caster sugar
3½ cups (875ml) milk
1 teaspoon vanilla extract
½ cup (80g) sultanas
ground nutmeg or ground cinnamon

1 Preheat oven to 160°C/140°C fan-forced.
2 Trim crusts from bread, butter each slice; cut each slice into four triangles. Arrange two rows of triangles, butter-side up, overlapping slightly, along base of shallow 2-litre (8-cup) ovenproof dish. Centre another row of triangles over first two rows, with triangles facing in opposite direction to triangles in first layer.
3 Whisk eggs, sugar, milk and extract in bowl. Pour half the custard mixture over bread; stand 10 minutes.
4 Whisk remaining custard mixture, add sultanas; pour into dish. Sprinkle with nutmeg or cinnamon. Stand dish in larger baking dish with enough boiling water to come halfway up side of dish.
5 Bake about 50 minutes or until custard is set.

prep + cook time 1 hour 10 minutes **serves** 4
tips This recipe can be made a day ahead; store, covered, in the refrigerator. Substitute any dried fruit of your choice in this recipe. This pudding is good, either hot or cold, with stewed fruit and ice-cream.

chocolate bread and butter pudding

1½ cups (375ml) milk
2 cups (500ml) cream
⅓ cup (75g) caster sugar
1 vanilla bean
4 eggs
2 small brioche (200g), sliced thickly
100g dark eating chocolate, chopped coarsely
⅓ cup (40g) coarsely chopped roasted pecans

1 Preheat oven to 180°C/160°C fan-forced.
2 Combine milk, cream and sugar in small saucepan. Split vanilla
bean in half lengthways; scrape seeds into pan then place pod in pan.
Stir over heat until hot; strain into large heatproof jug, discard pod.
3 Whisk eggs in large bowl; whisking constantly, pour hot milk mixture
into eggs.
4 Grease shallow 2-litre (8-cup) ovenproof dish; layer brioche, chocolate
and nuts, overlapping brioche slightly, in dish. Pour hot milk mixture
over brioche.
5 Place dish in large baking dish; add enough boiling water to come
halfway up sides of dish. Bake about 45 minutes or until pudding sets.
Remove pudding from baking dish; stand 5 minutes before serving.

prep + cook time 1 hour 10 minutes **serves** 6

white choc and raspberry croissant pudding

5 croissants (300g), sliced thinly
⅓ cup (110g) raspberry jam
100g white eating chocolate, chopped coarsely
1 cup (135g) raspberries
custard
1½ cups (375ml) cream
1¼ cups (310ml) milk
⅓ cup (75g) caster sugar
1 teaspoon vanilla extract
4 eggs

1 Preheat oven to 160°C/140°C fan-forced.
2 Make custard.
3 Grease shallow 2-litre (8-cup) ovenproof dish. Layer croissant slices, overlapping slightly, in dish; dollop spoonfuls of jam over slices. Sprinkle with chocolate and berries. Pour custard over the top.
4 Place dish in large baking dish; add enough boiling water to come halfway up sides of ovenproof dish. Bake about 1 hour or until pudding sets. Remove pudding from baking dish; stand 5 minutes before serving.
custard Combine cream, milk, sugar and extract in medium saucepan; bring to the boil. Whisk eggs in large bowl; whisking constantly, gradually add hot milk mixture to egg mixture.

prep + cook time 1 hour 15 minutes **serves** 8
tips Any type of berries, fresh or frozen, can be used instead of the raspberries in this pudding. You can use dark or milk eating chocolate in place of the white chocolate. Sprinkle the pudding with icing sugar and serve with a good quality ice-cream for a truly indulgent dessert.

heavenly bread and butter puddings

12 slices raisin bread
50g butter
⅔ cup (110g) seeded prunes,
  sliced
¼ cup (35g) finely chopped
  dried apricots
ground nutmeg

custard
2 eggs
½ cup (125ml) milk
½ cup (125ml) cream
¼ cup (55g) caster sugar
1 tablespoon Grand Marnier
citrus sauce
½ cup (125ml) marmalade
½ cup (125ml) water
1 tablespoon Grand Marnier
100g butter

1 Preheat oven to 160°C/140°C fan-forced. Grease four ¾-cup (180ml) soufflé dishes; line bases with baking paper.
2 Cut bread into 12 x 8 cm rounds, spread both sides of bread with butter. Toast bread on both sides. Place toasted rounds in base of each dish, top with half the prunes and half the apricots. Repeat layering with toast, prunes and apricots, finishing with toast.
3 Make custard; slowly pour into dishes. Stand 5 minutes or until custard is absorbed
4 Place dishes in large baking dish; add enough boiling water to come halfway up sides of dishes.
5 Bake puddings about 30 minutes or until just set.
6 Meanwhile, make citrus sauce.
7 Run a thin-bladed knife around outside of puddings, turn onto oven tray; remove baking paper. Using large spatula, turn puddings over, brush tops with citrus sauce; sprinkle with nutmeg. Brown puddings under hot grill; serve with citrus sauce.
custard Whisk ingredients in jug until combined
citrus sauce Stir ingredients in medium saucepan over heat, without boiling, until marmalade is melted. Simmer, stirring, 3 minutes or until sauce thickens slightly; strain.

prep + cook time 1 hour **serves** 4

coconut bread pudding

2 eggs
1 tablespoon caster sugar
½ teaspoon coconut essence
⅓ cup (80ml) cream
1 cup (250ml) milk
1 slice white bread
1 tablespoon sultanas
1 tablespoon desiccated coconut

1 Preheat oven to 180°C/160°C fan-forced.
2 Whisk eggs, sugar and essence in bowl until combined; gradually whisk in cream and milk.
3 Remove and discard crusts from bread, cut bread into small cubes. Place bread cubes into a 3-cup (750ml) ovenproof dish, sprinkle evenly with sultanas; top with custard mixture.
4 Place dish in larger baking dish; add enough boiling water to come halfway up the sides of ovenproof dish.
5 Bake pudding 30 minutes. Sprinkle custard evenly with coconut; bake further 10 minutes or until pudding is set. Stand 5 minutes before serving. Serve warm or cold.

prep + cook time 45 minutes **serves** 4

banana caramel bread and butter pudding

2 cups (500ml) cream
1½ cups (375ml) milk
⅓ cup (75g) caster sugar
1 teaspoon vanilla extract
4 eggs
½ cup (200g) caramel Top 'n' Fill
¼ cup (60ml) cream, extra
2 large overripe bananas (460g), sliced thickly
1 small french bread stick (120g), sliced thickly

1 Preheat oven to 180°C/160°C fan-forced. Grease shallow 2-litre (8-cup) ovenproof dish.
2 Heat cream, milk, sugar and extract in medium saucepan. Whisk eggs in large bowl; gradually whisk in hot cream mixture.
3 Combine caramel mixture and extra cream in small saucepan; cook, stirring over low heat, until smooth.
4 Place banana, in single layer, into dish. Layer bread on top of banana, overlapping slices slightly; drizzle with caramel cream then pour hot cream mixture over bread, taking care not to dislodge slices.
5 Place dish in larger baking dish; add enough boiling water to come halfway up sides of dish. Bake about 1 hour 20 minutes or until pudding sets. Remove pudding from water; stand 5 minutes before serving.

prep + cook time 1 hour 30 minutes **serves** 6

white chocolate panna cotta with passionfruit sauce

300ml thickened cream
¾ cup (180ml) milk
150g white chocolate, chopped coarsely
⅓ cup (75g) caster sugar
2 teaspoons gelatine
1 tablespoon water
½ cup (125ml) passionfruit pulp
1 cup (250ml) sauternes-style dessert wine

1 Grease six ½-cup (125ml) non-metallic moulds.
2 Stir cream, milk, chocolate and 2 tablespoons of the sugar in small saucepan over heat, without boiling, until smooth.
3 Sprinkle gelatine over the water in small heatproof jug. Stand jug in small saucepan of simmering water; stir until gelatine dissolves. Stir into cream mixture.
4 Divide mixture among moulds; refrigerate, covered, about 3 hours or until set.
5 Meanwhile, bring passionfruit, wine and remaining sugar to the boil in small saucepan. Reduce heat; simmer, uncovered, without stirring, about 10 minutes or until passionfruit syrup reduces by a third. Cool.
6 Turn panna cotta onto serving plates; drizzle with passionfruit syrup.

prep + cook time 30 minutes (+ refrigeration) **serves** 6
tips Sauternes is a dessert wine from the region of the same name in western France – serve the remaining dessert wine with the panna cotta. You will need about six passionfruit for this recipe. Panna cotta can be made a day ahead; store, covered, in refrigerator. Wipe the outsides of panna cotta moulds with a hot cloth to make turning them out onto serving plates easier.

clove panna cotta with fresh figs

1 teaspoon whole cloves
300ml thickened cream
⅔ cup (160ml) milk
2 teaspoons gelatine
2 tablespoons caster sugar
½ teaspoon vanilla extract
4 medium fresh figs (240g)
2 tablespoons honey

1 Grease four ½-cup (125ml) moulds.
2 Place cloves, cream and milk in small saucepan; stand 10 minutes. Sprinkle gelatine and sugar over cream mixture; stir over low heat, without boiling, until gelatine and sugar dissolve. Stir in extract. Strain mixture into medium jug; cool to room temperature.
3 Divide mixture among moulds; cover, refrigerate 3 hours or until set.
4 Quarter figs. Stir honey in small saucepan until warm.
5 Turn panna cotta onto serving plates; serve with figs drizzled with warm honey.

prep + cook time 30 minutes (+ cooling and refrigeration) **serves** 4
tip Wipe the outsides of panna cotta moulds with a hot cloth to make turning them out onto serving plates easier.

passionfruit panna cotta with mango

1 cup (250ml) milk
300ml cream
⅓ cup (75g) caster sugar
⅓ cup (80ml) sieved passionfruit juice
2 teaspoons gelatine
2 tablespoons water
2 small mangoes (600g), sliced thinly
2 passionfruits

1 Stir milk, cream and sugar in medium saucepan over low heat until warm. Remove from heat, stir in juice; cool.
2 Sprinkle gelatine over the water in small heatproof jug. Stand jug in small saucepan of simmering water; stir until gelatine dissolves. Cool slightly then stir into cream mixture.
3 Divide mixture among six ½-cup (125ml) moulds. Cover; refrigerate about 3 hours or overnight.
4 Arrange mango on serving plates. Turn panna cotta onto mango; drizzle with passionfruit pulp.

prep + cook time 20 minutes (+ refrigeration) **serves** 6
tips You need about eight passionfruits for this recipe: six to sieve for the juice and two for the pulp topping. Wipe the outsides of panna cotta moulds with a hot cloth to make turning them out onto serving plates easier.

vanilla panna cotta with berry compote

2 tablespoons boiling water
2 tablespoons honey
1 vanilla bean
2 teaspoons gelatine
1½ cups (420g) yogurt
berry compote
2 cups (300g) frozen mixed berries
¼ cup (40g) icing sugar

1 Combine the water and honey in small heatproof jug. Split vanilla bean in half lengthways; scrape seeds into jug then place pod in jug. Sprinkle gelatine over honey mixture; stand jug in small saucepan of simmering water. Stir until gelatine dissolves; cool 5 minutes. Discard vanilla pod.
2 Combine honey mixture and yogurt in small bowl; stir until smooth. Strain mixture into four ½-cup (125ml) moulds, cover; refrigerate 3 hours or overnight.
3 Make berry compote.
4 Turn panna cotta onto serving plates; serve with berry compote.
berry compote Combine ingredients in medium saucepan over low heat, uncovered, stirring occasionally, about 5 minutes or until berries just soften. Transfer to small bowl; cool 10 minutes. Cover; refrigerate until required.

prep + cook time 25 minutes (+ refrigeration) **serves** 4
tips Panna cotta is usually made with milk, but in this recipe it's made with yogurt, which gives it a particularly creamy texture. Rather than serving with the berry compote, use any sliced fresh fruit you like; mango is particularly good, as are any of the summer stone fruits. Wipe the outsides of panna cotta moulds with a hot cloth to make turning them out onto serving plates easier.

citrus rice pudding

2 cups (500ml) no-fat milk
1 vanilla bean, halved lengthways
1 teaspoon finely grated lemon rind
1 teaspoon finely grated lime rind
2 teaspoons finely grated orange rind
2 eggs
1 egg white
½ cup (110g) caster sugar
1½ cups cooked white medium-grain rice
½ cup (125ml) low-fat cream

1 Preheat oven to 160°C/140°C fan-forced. Grease shallow oval 1.5-litre (6-cup) ovenproof dish.
2 Bring milk, vanilla bean and rinds to the boil in medium saucepan. Remove from heat; stand, covered, 5 minutes.
3 Meanwhile, whisk eggs, egg white and sugar in medium bowl. Gradually whisk hot milk mixture into egg mixture; discard vanilla bean.
4 Spread rice into dish; pour egg mixture carefully over rice. Place dish in large baking dish; add enough boiling water to baking dish to come halfway up side of pudding dish.
5 Bake pudding about 1 hour or until set. Serve warm with cream.

prep + cook time 1 hour 20 minutes **serves** 8
tip You need to cook about ½ cup (100g) white medium-grain rice for this recipe.

coconut rice puddings

4 eggs
⅓ cup (75g) caster sugar
1 teaspoon vanilla extract
400ml can coconut cream
1½ cups (375ml) gluten-free soy milk
1 cup cooked white medium-grain rice
½ cup (80g) sultanas
½ teaspoon ground cinnamon

1 Preheat oven to 180°C/160°C fan-forced. Grease six ¾-cup (180ml) ovenproof dishes.
2 Whisk eggs, sugar and extract in large jug until combined; whisk in cream and soy milk. Stir in rice and sultanas. Divide mixture evenly among dishes; place dishes in large baking dish. Add enough boiling water to come halfway up sides of small dishes.
3 Bake puddings 20 minutes, whisking gently with fork under the skin of the puddings twice – this stops the rice sinking to the bottom of the dishes. Sprinkle puddings with cinnamon; bake further 20 minutes or until set. Stand puddings 10 minutes before serving.

prep + cook time 1 hour **makes** 6
tips You will need to cook ⅓ cup (65g) white medium-grain rice for this recipe. Puddings can be stored, covered, in the refrigerator for up to 2 days.

white chocolate and black cherry creamed rice

1.5 litres (6 cups) milk
⅔ cup (130g) arborio rice
2 tablespoons caster sugar
90g white chocolate, chopped finely
425g can seedless black cherries, drained

1 Bring milk, rice, sugar and half the chocolate to the boil in medium saucepan. Reduce heat; simmer over very low heat, stirring often, about 40 minutes or until rice is tender.
2 Serve rice warm, topped with cherries and remaining chocolate. Serve sprinkled with nutmeg, if you like.

prep + cook time 50 minutes **serves** 6
tip We used arborio rice in this recipe but you could use calrose, a white medium-grain rice, instead.

baked rice custard

4 eggs
⅓ cup (75g) caster sugar
½ teaspoon vanilla extract
2 cups (500ml) milk
300ml cream
⅓ cup (50g) raisins
1½ cups cold cooked white medium-grain rice
1 teaspoon ground cinnamon

1 Preheat oven to 180°C/160°C fan-forced. Grease 1.5-litre (6-cup) baking dish.
2 Whisk eggs, sugar and extract in medium bowl until combined. Whisk in milk and cream; stir in raisins and rice. Pour mixture into dish.
3 Place dish in larger baking dish; pour enough boiling water into baking dish to come halfway up sides of dish.
4 Bake custard 30 minutes, whisking lightly with fork under skin occasionally. Sprinkle with cinnamon; bake further 20 minutes. Serve warm or cold.

prep + cook time 1 hour **serves** 6
tip You need to cook about ½ cup (100g) white medium-grain rice for this recipe.

creamed rice

1 litre (4 cups) milk
⅓ cup (75g) caster sugar
1 teaspoon vanilla extract
½ cup (100g) white medium-grain rice

1 Bring milk, sugar and extract to the boil in large saucepan; gradually add rice to boiling milk. Reduce heat; simmer, covered, stirring occasionally, about 50 minutes or until rice is tender and milk is almost absorbed.
2 Serve warm or cold, with fresh berries, if desired.

prep + cook time 55 minutes **serves** 4

crème brûlée

1 vanilla bean
3 cups (750ml) thickened cream
6 egg yolks
¼ cup (55g) caster sugar
¼ cup (40g) pure icing sugar

1 Preheat oven to 180°C/160°C fan-forced. Grease six ½-cup (125ml) ovenproof dishes.
2 Split vanilla bean in half lengthways; scrape seeds into medium heatproof bowl. Place pod in small saucepan, add cream and heat without boiling.
3 Add egg yolks and caster sugar to seeds in bowl; gradually whisk in hot cream mixture. Set bowl over medium saucepan of simmering water; stir over heat about 10 minutes or until custard mixture thickens slightly and coats the back of a spoon; discard pod.
4 Place dishes in large baking dish; divide custard among dishes. Add enough boiling water to baking dish to come halfway up sides of ovenproof dishes.
5 Bake custards about 20 minutes or until custard sets. Remove custards from dish; cool. Cover; refrigerate overnight.
6 Preheat grill. Place custards in shallow flameproof dish filled with ice cubes. Sprinkle each custard evenly with sifted icing sugar; using finger, gently smooth over the surface of each custard. Place dish under grill until sugar caramelises.

prep + cook time 1 hour (+ refrigeration) **serves** 6

passionfruit and coconut crème brûlée

2 eggs
4 egg yolks
¼ cup (55g) caster sugar
½ cup (125ml) passionfruit pulp
1⅔ cups (400ml) coconut cream
300ml thickened cream
2 tablespoons brown sugar

1 Preheat oven to 180°C/160°C fan-forced.
2 Combine eggs, egg yolks, caster sugar and passionfruit in medium heatproof bowl.
3 Bring coconut cream and cream to the boil in small saucepan. Gradually whisk hot cream mixture into egg mixture. Place bowl over medium saucepan of simmering water; stir over heat about 10 minutes or until custard mixture thickens slightly and coats the back of a spoon.
4 Divide custard among eight ½-cup (125ml) heatproof dishes or cups. Place dishes in large baking dish. Pour enough boiling water into baking dish to come halfway up sides of dishes.
5 Bake custards about 20 minutes or until custards just set. Remove custards from water; cool to room temperature. Cover; refrigerate 3 hours or overnight.
6 Preheat grill. Place custards in shallow flameproof dish filled with ice cubes. Sprinkle each custard with 1 teaspoon brown sugar; using finger, gently smooth over the surface of each custard. Place dish under grill until sugar caramelises.

prep + cook time 1 hour (+ refrigeration) **serves** 8
tip You will need about six passionfruit for this recipe.

passionfruit and lime crème brûlée

¼ cup (60ml) passionfruit pulp
1 egg
2 egg yolks
2 tablespoons caster sugar
1 teaspoon finely grated lime rind
280ml can coconut cream
½ cup (125ml) gluten-free soy milk
1 tablespoon brown sugar

1 Preheat oven to 180°C/160°C fan-forced.
2 Combine passionfruit, egg, egg yolks, caster sugar and rind in medium heatproof bowl.
3 Bring coconut cream and milk to the boil in small saucepan. Gradually whisk hot cream mixture into egg mixture. Place bowl over medium saucepan of simmering water; stir over heat about 10 minutes or until custard thickens slightly.
4 Divide custard among four deep ½-cup (125ml) heatproof dishes. Place dishes in medium baking dish; pour enough boiling water into baking dish to come halfway up sides of dishes.
5 Bake custard about 40 minutes or until custard is set. Remove custards from water; cool. Cover; refrigerate 3 hours or overnight.
6 Preheat grill. Place custards in shallow flameproof dish filled with ice cubes. Sprinkle each custard with 1 teaspoon brown sugar; using finger, gently smooth sugar over the surface of each custard. Place dish under grill until sugar caramelises.

prep + cook time 1 hour (+ cooling and refrigeration) **serves** 4
tip This recipe is gluten-free, wheat-free, yeast-free, dairy-free and nut-free.

coffee crème caramels

¾ cup (165g) caster sugar
¾ cup (180ml) water
6 eggs
⅓ cup (75g) caster sugar, extra
2 tablespoons coffee-flavoured liqueur
1 tablespoon instant coffee granules
1 tablespoon water, extra
1½ cups (375ml) milk
300ml thickened cream

1 Preheat oven to 160°C/140°C fan-forced.
2 Stir sugar and the water in medium saucepan over heat, without boiling, until sugar is dissolved. Bring to the boil; boil, uncovered, without stirring, about 5 minutes or until mixture is golden brown. Pour evenly into six 1-cup (250ml) ovenproof dishes.
3 Whisk eggs and extra sugar together in medium bowl; stir in liqueur and combined coffee and extra water.
4 Bring milk and cream to the boil in medium saucepan. Remove from heat; allow bubbles to subside. Gradually whisk milk mixture into egg mixture; strain into jug.
5 Place dishes in baking dish; pour custard into dishes. Pour enough boiling water into baking dish to come halfway up sides of dishes.
6 Bake crème caramels 30 minutes or until just set. Remove dishes from water; cool to room temperature. Refrigerate overnight.
7 Turn crème caramels onto serving plates, serve with extra whipped cream and orange rind, if you like.

prep + cook time 50 minutes (+ refrigeration) **serves** 6

ginger crème caramels

¾ cup (165g) caster sugar
¾ cup (180ml) water
2 tablespoons finely chopped glacé ginger
4 eggs
1 teaspoon vanilla extract
¼ cup (55g) caster sugar, extra
1¼ cups (310ml) milk
¾ cup (180ml) thickened cream

1 Preheat oven to 180°C/160°C fan-forced.
2 Stir sugar, the water and ginger in medium saucepan over heat, without boiling, until sugar is dissolved. Bring to the boil; boil, uncovered, without stirring, 2 minutes; strain sugar syrup. Return sugar syrup to same pan, return to boil; boil, uncovered, without stirring about 3 minutes or until golden brown. Pour evenly into six ¾-cup (180ml) ovenproof dishes.
3 Whisk eggs, extract and extra sugar in medium bowl.
4 Bring milk and cream to the boil in medium saucepan. Remove from heat; allow bubbles to subside. Gradually whisk milk mixture into egg mixture; strain into jug.
5 Place dishes into baking dish; pour custard into dishes. Pour enough boiling water into baking dish to come halfway up sides of dishes.
6 Bake crème caramels 20 minutes or until just set. Remove dishes from water; cool to room temperature. Refrigerate overnight. Turn crème caramels onto serving plates, serve with extra glacé ginger and strawberries, if you like.

prep + cook time 45 minutes (+ refrigeration) **serves** 6
tip This recipe is best made a day ahead; store, covered, in refrigerator.

crème caramel

¾ cup (165g) caster sugar
½ cup (125ml) water
300ml cream
1¾ cups (430ml) milk
6 eggs
1 teaspoon vanilla extract
⅓ cup (75g) caster sugar, extra

1 Preheat oven to 160°C/140°C fan-forced.
2 Stir sugar and the water in medium frying pan over heat, without boiling, until sugar dissolves. Bring to the boil; boil, uncovered, without stirring, until mixture is deep caramel in colour. Remove from heat; allow bubbles to subside. Pour toffee into deep 20cm-round cake pan.
3 Bring cream and milk to the boil in medium saucepan. Whisk eggs, extract and extra sugar in large bowl; whisking constantly, pour hot milk mixture into egg mixture. Strain mixture into cake pan.
4 Place pan in medium baking dish; add enough boiling water to come half way up side of pan.
5 Bake crème caramel about 40 minutes or until firm. Remove pan from baking dish, cover; refrigerate overnight.
6 Gently ease crème caramel from side of pan; invert onto deep-sided serving plate.

prep + cook time 1 hour (+ refrigeration) **serves** 6

cinnamon flan

1 cup (220g) caster sugar
½ cup (125ml) water
2½ cups (625ml) milk
300ml thickened cream
2 cinnamon sticks
2 cloves
4 eggs
2 egg yolks
⅓ cup (75g) caster sugar, extra
2 teaspoons vanilla extract

1 Preheat oven to 160°C/140°C fan-forced.
2 Stir sugar and the water in medium heavy-based saucepan over heat, without boiling, until sugar dissolves; bring to the boil. Reduce heat; simmer, uncovered, without stirring, until syrup is golden brown in colour. Pour syrup over base of deep 20cm-round cake pan. Place pan in large baking dish (toffee will set at this stage).
3 Bring milk, cream and spices to the boil in medium saucepan. Remove from heat, cover; stand 15 minutes. Strain milk mixture; discard spices.
4 Whisk eggs, egg yolks, extra sugar and extract in medium bowl. Gradually whisk warm milk mixture into egg mixture; strain mixture over toffee in pan. Pour enough boiling water into baking dish to come halfway up side of pan.
5 Bake custard about 45 minutes or until custard just sets. Remove pan from water; cool. Cover; refrigerate 24 hours.
6 Just before serving, turn flan onto a rimmed serving dish.

prep + cook time 1 hour (+ standing and refrigeration) **serves** 8
tip This recipe must be made 24 hours ahead to allow toffee to dissolve.

baked chocolate custard

3 eggs
¼ cup (25g) cocoa powder
⅓ cup (75g) caster sugar
2 cups (500ml) milk
1 tablespoon icing sugar

1 Preheat oven to 180°C/160°C fan-forced.
2 Whisk eggs, sifted cocoa and sugar together in large bowl.
3 Heat milk in small saucepan; gradually whisk into egg mixture.
Pour mixture into four ¾-cup (180ml) ovenproof dishes.
4 Place dishes in baking dish; add enough water to come halfway up
sides of dishes.
5 Bake custards 45 minutes or until set. Dust with sifted icing sugar
just before serving.

prep + cook time 1 hour **serves** 4

nougat almond custard

30g butter
70g packet dessert nougat
½ cup (110g) caster sugar
¼ cup (60ml) water
1 egg
3 egg yolks
1½ tablespoons almond-flavoured liqueur
1 teaspoon gelatine
1 tablespoon water, extra
300ml thickened cream

1 Melt butter in medium saucepan, add nougat; stir over heat, without boiling, until nougat is melted. Stir in sugar and the water over heat, without boiling, until sugar is dissolved. Bring to the boil; boil, uncovered, without stirring, about 3 minutes or until syrup is thickened slightly.
2 Beat egg and egg yolks in small bowl with electric mixer until thick and creamy; beat in liqueur. With motor operating, gradually add hot nougat syrup.
3 Sprinkle gelatine over extra water in small bowl; stand in small saucepan of simmering water, stir until dissolved, cool slightly. Gradually beat gelatine mixture into nougat mixture. Transfer mixture to large bowl.
4 Beat cream in small bowl until soft peaks form; fold into nougat mixture. Pour mixture into six ⅔-cup (160ml) serving glasses. Decorate with toffee pieces, if you like.

prep + cook time 1 hour **serves** 6

baked custard

6 eggs
1 teaspoon vanilla extract
⅓ cup (75g) caster sugar
1 litre (4 cups) hot milk
¼ teaspoon ground nutmeg

1 Preheat oven to 160°C/140°C fan-forced. Grease shallow 1.5-litre (6-cup) ovenproof dish.
2 Whisk eggs, extract and sugar in large bowl; gradually whisk in hot milk. Pour custard mixture into dish; sprinkle with nutmeg.
3 Place dish in larger baking dish; add enough boiling water to come halfway up sides of dish.
4 Bake custard about 45 minutes. Remove custard from large dish; stand 5 minutes before serving.

prep + cook time 55 minutes **serves** 6

fruit mince and brioche pudding

475g jar fruit mince
2 tablespoons brandy
300g brioche, sliced thickly
1 tablespoon demerara sugar
custard
1½ cups (375ml) milk
2 cups (500ml) cream
⅓ cup (75g) caster sugar
½ teaspoon vanilla extract
4 eggs

1 Preheat oven to 160°C/140°C fan-forced. Grease shallow 2-litre (8-cup) ovenproof dish.
2 Make custard.
3 Combine fruit mince and brandy in small bowl. Layer brioche and half the fruit mixture, overlapping brioche slightly, in dish. Dollop spoonfuls of remaining fruit mixture over brioche. Pour custard over brioche; sprinkle with sugar.
4 Place dish in large baking dish; add enough boiling water to come halfway up sides of dish.
5 Bake pudding about 45 minutes or until set. Remove pudding from baking dish; stand 5 minutes before serving.
custard Bring milk, cream, sugar and extract to the boil in medium saucepan. Whisk eggs in large bowl; whisking constantly, gradually add hot milk mixture to egg mixture.

prep + cook time 1 hour **serves** 6

queen of puddings

2 cups (140g) stale breadcrumbs
1 tablespoon caster sugar
1 teaspoon vanilla extract
1 teaspoon finely grated lemon rind
2½ cups (625ml) milk
60g butter
4 eggs, separated
¼ cup (80g) raspberry jam, warmed
¾ cup (165g) caster sugar, extra

1 Preheat oven to 180°C/160°C fan-forced. Grease six ¾-cup (180ml) ovenproof dishes; stand on oven tray.
2 Combine breadcrumbs, sugar, extract and rind in large bowl. Heat milk and butter in medium saucepan until almost boiling, pour over bread mixture; stand 10 minutes. Stir in yolks.
3 Divide mixture among dishes. Bake about 30 minutes. Carefully spread top of hot puddings with jam.
4 Beat egg whites in small bowl with electric mixer until soft peaks form; gradually add extra sugar, beating until sugar dissolves. Spoon meringue over puddings; bake about 10 minutes.

prep + cook time 55 minutes **serves** 6

STEAMED PUDDINGS

steamed christmas pudding

3 cups (450g) chopped mixed
  dried fruit
¾ cup (120g) finely chopped
  dried seedless dates
¾ cup (120g) finely chopped
  raisins
¾ cup (180ml) water
1 cup (220g) firmly packed
  brown sugar

100g butter, chopped
1 teaspoon bicarbonate of soda
2 eggs, beaten lightly
¾ cup (110g) plain flour
¾ cup (110g) self-raising flour
1 teaspoon mixed spice
½ teaspoon ground cinnamon
2 tablespoons dark rum

1 Stir fruit, the water, sugar and butter in medium saucepan over medium heat until butter melts and sugar dissolves; bring to the boil. Reduce heat; simmer, uncovered, 6 minutes. Stir in soda. Transfer mixture to large bowl; cool to room temperature.

2 Stir eggs, sifted dry ingredients and rum into fruit mixture.

3 Grease 2 litre (8 cup) pudding steamer; spoon mixture into steamer. Top with pleated baking paper and foil (to allow pudding to expand as it cooks); secure with kitchen string or lid.

4 Place pudding in large boiler with enough boiling water to come halfway up side of steamer. Cover with tight-fitting lid; boil for 4 hours, replenishing water as necessary to maintain level. Stand pudding 10 minutes before turning onto plate; serve with cream, if desired.

prep + cook time 4 hours 30 minutes (+ cooling)

tips To store pudding, allow pudding to come to room temperature then wrap pudding in plastic wrap; refrigerate in cleaned steamer, or seal tightly in freezer bag or airtight container. Pudding can be stored in refrigerator up to two months or frozen up to 12 months.

To reheat, thaw frozen pudding three days in refrigerator; remove from refrigerator 12 hours before reheating. Remove from plastic wrap and return to steamer. Steam 2 hours following instructions in step 4.

To reheat in microwave oven, reheat up to four single serves at once. Cover with plastic wrap; microwave on HIGH (100%) up to 1 minute per serve. To reheat whole pudding, cover with plastic wrap; microwave on MEDIUM (55%) about 15 minutes or until hot.

college pudding

⅓ cup (110g) raspberry jam
1 egg
½ cup (110g) caster sugar
1 cup (150g) self-raising flour
½ cup (125ml) milk
25g butter, melted
1 tablespoon boiling water
1 teaspoon vanilla extract

1 Grease four 1-cup (250ml) metal moulds; divide jam among moulds.
2 Beat egg and sugar in small bowl with electric mixer until thick and creamy. Fold in sifted flour and milk, in two batches; fold in combined butter, the water and extract.
3 Top jam with pudding mixture. Cover each mould with pleated baking paper and foil (to allow puddings to expand as they cook); secure with kitchen string.
4 Place puddings in large saucepan with enough boiling water to come halfway up sides of moulds. Cover pan with tight-fitting lid; boil 25 minutes, replenishing water as necessary to maintain level. Stand puddings 5 minutes before turning onto plate. Serve with cream.

prep + cook time 40 minutes **serves** 4

steamed ginger pudding

60g butter
¼ cup (90g) golden syrup
½ teaspoon bicarbonate of soda
1 cup (150g) self-raising flour
2 teaspoons ground ginger
½ cup (125ml) milk
1 egg
syrup
⅓ cup (115g) golden syrup
2 tablespoons water
30g butter

1 Grease 1.25-litre (5-cup) pudding steamer.
2 Stir butter and syrup in small saucepan over low heat until smooth. Remove from heat, stir in soda; transfer mixture to medium bowl. Stir in sifted dry ingredients then combined milk and egg, in two batches.
3 Spread mixture into steamer. Cover with pleated baking paper and foil (to allow pudding to expand as it cooks); secure with lid.
4 Place pudding steamer in large saucepan with enough boiling water to come halfway up side of steamer; cover pan with tight-fitting lid. Boil 1 hour, replenishing water as necessary to maintain level. Stand pudding 5 minutes before turning onto plate.
5 Meanwhile, make syrup.
6 Serve pudding topped with syrup and, if desired, cream.
syrup Stir ingredients in small saucepan over heat until smooth; bring to the boil. Reduce heat; simmer, uncovered, 2 minutes.

prep + cook time 1 hour **serves** 6

tangelo syrup pudding

2 large tangelos (420g)
125g butter
½ cup (110g) caster sugar
2 eggs
1 cup (150g) wholemeal self-raising flour
½ cup (75g) white self-raising flour
½ teaspoon bicarbonate of soda
¼ cup (60ml) buttermilk
syrup
½ cup (110g) caster sugar
60g butter

1 Grease 1.75-litre (7-cup) pudding steamer; line base with baking paper.
2 Squeeze juice from tangelos, reserve juice for syrup; you will need
⅔ cup juice. Blend or process remaining skin and pulp until smooth.
3 Beat butter and sugar in small bowl with electric mixer until light and
fluffy. Beat in eggs, one at a time, beating until combined between
additions. Stir in sifted dry ingredients and buttermilk, in two batches.
Stir in pureed tangelo pulp. Spread mixture into steamer, cover with
pleated baking paper and foil; secure with string or cover with lid.
4 Place steamer in large saucepan with enough boiling water to come
halfway up side of basin; cover with tight-fitting lid. Boil 1½ hours,
replenishing water as necessary to maintain level.
5 Make syrup.
6 Stand wire rack over shallow tray, turn pudding onto rack, pour hot
syrup over pudding. Serve pudding with any remaining syrup and cream.
syrup Stir sugar, reserved juice and butter in small saucepan over heat,
without boiling, until sugar is dissolved; bring to the boil. Reduce heat,
simmer, uncovered, without stirring, 3 minutes.

prep + cook time 2 hours **serves** 8
tip Tangelos are a citrus fruit that's a cross between a mandarin and
grapefruit. They not only taste good but have a wonderful colour.

chocolate bread pudding with brandy cream

150g butter
¾ cup (165g) caster sugar
1 tablespoon brandy
5 eggs, beaten lightly
1¼ cups (150g) ground almonds
375g dark eating chocolate, chopped finely
2½ cups (250g) stale breadcrumbs
¼ cup (35g) cornflour
2 tablespoons cocoa powder
brandy cream
1½ cups (375ml) milk
1 vanilla bean
4 egg yolks
⅓ cup (75g) caster sugar
1 teaspoon cornflour
2 tablespoons brandy

1 Grease 1.5-litre (6-cup) pudding steamer.
2 Beat butter, sugar and brandy in small bowl with electric mixer until light and fluffy. Gradually beat in egg (mixture will curdle at this stage). Transfer mixture to large bowl; stir in ground almonds, chocolate, breadcrumbs and sifted cornflour and cocoa.
3 Spread mixture into steamer. Cover with pleated baking paper and foil; secure with string or lid. Place steamer in large saucepan with enough boiling water to come halfway up side of steamer; cover pan with tight-fitting lid. Boil 2¼ hours or until firm, replenishing water as necessary to maintain level. Stand pudding for 5 minutes before turning out.
4 Meanwhile, make brandy cream. Serve hot pudding with brandy cream.
brandy cream Bring milk and vanilla bean to the boil in small saucepan. Reduce heat; simmer, uncovered, 5 minutes. Remove from heat, cool, strain; remove bean, wash and reserve for future use. Combine egg yolks, sugar and cornflour in medium heatproof bowl over medium saucepan of simmering water; stir in milk until mixture thickens slightly. Stir in brandy.

prep + cook time 2 hours 45 minutes **serves** 8

steamed pumpkin and maple pudding

1 cup mashed cooked pumpkin
½ cup (125ml) milk
90g butter, melted
2 eggs, beaten lightly
2 tablespoons honey
1 cup (220g) firmly packed brown sugar
2 cups (300g) self-raising flour
½ teaspoon bicarbonate of soda
1 teaspoon ground cinnamon
½ teaspoon ground nutmeg
½ cup (70g) slivered almonds
½ cup (125ml) maple syrup

1 Grease 2-litre (8-cup) pudding steamer.
2 Combine pumpkin, milk, butter, egg, honey and sugar in medium bowl. Stir in sifted dry ingredients and almonds.
3 Pour mixture into steamer. Cover with pleated baking paper and foil; secure with string or lid.
4 Place steamer in large saucepan with enough boiling water to come halfway up side of steamer; cover pan with tight-fitting lid. Boil about 1½ hours or until firm, replenishing water as necessary to maintain level. Turn pudding onto serving plate; serve with maple syrup and cream

prep + cook time 2 hours **serves** 8
tips You will need to cook 350g pumpkin for the amount of mashed pumpkin required in this recipe. Pudding can be made a day ahead; store in airtight container. Pudding can be frozen for 2 months.

chocolate chip pudding

125g butter, chopped
2 teaspoons grated orange rind
1 cup (220g) caster sugar
4 eggs
½ cup (60g) ground almonds
½ cup (125ml) orange juice
½ cup (60g) stale cake crumbs
1 cup (150g) self-raising flour
1 cup (150g) plain flour
¾ cup (140g) Choc Bits
chocolate sauce
½ cup (125ml) thickened cream
100g dark eating chocolate, chopped

1 Grease 1.5-litre (6-cup) pudding steamer.
2 Beat butter, rind and sugar in small bowl with electric mixer until light and fluffy. Beat in eggs, one at a time (mixture might curdle at this stage); transfer mixture to large bowl. Stir in ground almonds, juice, crumbs and sifted flours in two batches; stir in Choc Bits.
3 Spoon mixture into steamer. Cover with pleated baking paper and foil; secure with string or lid. Place steamer in large saucepan with enough boiling water to come halfway up side of steamer; cover with tight-fitting lid. Boil about 2 hours or until firm, replenishing water as necessary to maintain level.
4 Make chcoolate sauce. Serve pudding hot with sauce.
chocolate sauce Stir cream and chocolate in small saucepan over heat, without boiling, until mixture is smooth and heated through.

prep + cook time 2 hours 20 minutes **serves** 8
tip Pudding can be made an day ahead; keep, covered, in refrigerator or freeze for 3 months.

steamed chocolate and golden syrup pudding

185g butter
½ cup (100g) firmly packed brown sugar
½ cup (125ml) golden syrup
¼ cup (60ml) honey
¼ cup (60ml) water
2 eggs, beaten lightly
1½ cups (225g) plain flour
1½ cups (225g) self-raising flour
2 tablespoons cocoa powder
1 teaspoon bicarbonate of soda
butterscotch sauce
50g butter
300ml thickened cream
1 cup (200g) firmly packed brown sugar
2 teaspoons vanilla extract

1 Grease 1.75-litre (7-cup) pudding steamer, line base with baking paper.
2 Stir butter, sugar, syrup, honey and the water in medium saucepan over heat until butter melts and sugar dissolves. Bring to the boil, remove from heat; cool. Stir in eggs then sifted dry ingredients. Spoon pudding mixture into prepared steamer; cover pudding with greased foil, secure with lid or kitchen string.
3 Place steamer in large saucepan with enough boiling water to come halfway up side of steamer; simmer, covered, about 2 hours or until pudding is firm, replenishing water as necessary to maintain level.
4 Make butterscotch sauce.
5 Serve pudding with sauce.
butterscotch sauce Stir ingredients in medium saucepan, over heat until butter melts. Simmer, uncovered, about 5 minutes or until sauce thickens slightly.

prep + cook time 2 hours 30 minutes **serves** 8

chocolate hazelnut steamed pudding

4 eggs
1 cup (220g) caster sugar
125g unsalted butter, chopped
1 cup (100g) ground hazelnuts
200g dark chocolate, grated coarsely
2 cups (140g) stale breadcrumbs
½ cup (75g) self-raising flour
coffee cream
300ml thickened cream
1 egg, beaten lightly
2 tablespoons coffee-flavoured liqueur
1 tablespoon caster sugar

1 Grease 1.5-litre (6-cup) pudding steamer.
2 Beat eggs and sugar in small bowl with electric mixer until light and fluffy. Add butter gradually to egg mixture; beat until just combined. Transfer mixture to large bowl; fold in ground nuts, chocolate, breadcrumbs and sifted flour.
3 Spoon mixture into steamer; cover with pleated baking paper and foil; secure with string or lid. Place steamer in large saucepan with enough boiling water to come halfway up side of steamer; cover with tight-fitting lid. Simmer about 2½ hours or until firm, replenishing water as necessary to maintain level.
4 Make coffee cream.
5 Serve pudding hot with coffee cream.
coffee cream Stir ingredients in small saucepan, constantly, over low heat, without boiling, until thickened slightly; strain before serving.

prep + cook time 3 hours **serves** 8
tip This pudding is best prepared as close to serving time as possible.

quince and spice steamed pudding with orange syrup

800g quinces
½ cup (125ml) water
1 tablespoon brown sugar
2 teaspoons finely grated
orange rind
100g butter
½ cup (110g) firmly packed
brown sugar, extra
2 eggs
1½ cups (225g) self-raising flour
½ teaspoon bicarbonate of soda

2 teaspoons ground ginger
1 teaspoon mixed spice
½ cup (125ml) milk
orange syrup
1 medium orange (240g)
1 cup (220g) caster sugar
1½ cups (375ml) water
6 cardamom pods, bruised
1 cinnamon stick
2 star anise

1 Grease 1.5-litre (6-cup) pudding basin.
2 Peel quinces; cut into quarters, core, then chop fruit coarsely. Place quince in large saucepan with the water, sugar and rind; cook, covered, over low heat, stirring occasionally, about 30 minutes or until quince softens. Cool to room temperature.
3 Beat butter and extra sugar in small bowl with electric mixer until light and fluffy. Beat in eggs, one at a time, beating until combined between additions. Stir in sifted flour, soda, ginger and spice until smooth; stir in milk and cooled quince mixture. Spread mixture into basin. Cover with pleated baking paper and foil; secure with lid.
4 Place basin in large saucepan with enough boiling water to come halfway up side of basin; cover pan with tight-fitting lid. Boil 1½ hours, replenishing water as necessary. Stand 5 minutes before turning onto plate.
5 Meanwhile, make orange syrup.
6 Pour half of the syrup over hot pudding. Serve pudding with remaining syrup and, if desired, whipped cream.
orange syrup Using knife, cut rind from orange; cut rind into thin strips. Squeeze juice from orange (you need ⅓ cup). Stir rind and juice in small saucepan with remaining ingredients over heat, without boiling, until sugar dissolves. Reduce heat; simmer, uncovered, without stirring, about 10 minutes or until syrup thickens slightly. Discard spices.

prep + cook time 2 hours 30 minutes **serves** 8

steamed date pudding

3 cups (420g) coarsely chopped dried dates
90g butter
¾ cup (165g) firmly packed brown sugar
¾ cup (180ml) water
1 tablespoon malt vinegar
2 eggs
1 tablespoon brandy
2 cups (300g) plain flour
½ cup (75g) self-raising flour
1 teaspoon bicarbonate of soda
1 teaspoon ground cinnamon
1 teaspoon mixed spice
½ cup (125ml) milk

1 Grease 2-litre (8-cup) pudding steamer.
2 Stir dates, butter, sugar and the water in medium saucepan, over heat, without boiling, until butter is melted and sugar dissolved; bring to the boil. Reduce heat; simmer, uncovered, 5 minutes. Stir in vinegar; cool to room temperature.
3 Stir eggs and brandy into date mixture, then stir in sifted dry ingredients and milk, in two batches. Spoon mixture into steamer; cover with greased foil, secure with string or lid.
4 Place steamer in large saucepan with enough boiling water to come halfway up side of steamer; cover with tight-fitting lid. Boil about 2 hours, replenishing water as necessary to maintain level.
5 Serve pudding warm with custard or cream.

prep + cook time 3 hours (+ cooling) **serves** 10

MOUSSES

chocolate mousse

200g dark eating chocolate, chopped coarsely
30g unsalted butter
3 eggs, separated
300ml thickened cream, whipped

1 Melt chocolate in medium heatproof bowl over medium saucepan
of simmering water. Remove from heat; add butter, stir until smooth.
Stir in egg yolks. Transfer mixture to large bowl, cover; cool.
2 Beat egg whites in small bowl with electric mixer until soft peaks form.
Fold egg whites and cream into chocolate mixture, in two batches.
3 Divide mousse among six ¾-cup (180ml) serving dishes; refrigerate
3 hours or overnight. Serve with extra whipped cream, chocolate curls
and fresh raspberries.

prep + cook time 25 minutes (+ cooling and refrigeration) **serves** 6
tip This recipe can be made up to 2 days ahead; store, covered,
in refrigerator.

chocolate mousse cake with coffee anglaise

6 eggs, separated
½ cup (80g) icing sugar
¼ cup (25g) cocoa powder
2 tablespoons cornflour
150g dark eating chocolate,
   melted
1 tablespoon water
1 litre (4 cups) thickened cream
600g dark eating chocolate,
   melted, extra

coffee anglaise
3 cups (750ml) milk
1½ cups (135g) coffee beans
8 egg yolks
¾ cup (165g) caster sugar

1 Make coffee anglaise.
2 Preheat oven to 180°C/160°C fan-forced. Grease 25cm x 30cm swiss roll pan; cover base and short sides of pan with baking paper, bringing paper 5cm above edges.
3 Beat egg yolks and icing sugar in small bowl with electric mixer until light and creamy. Transfer to large bowl. Fold in sifted cocoa powder and cornflour, then chocolate; stir in the water.
4 Beat egg whites in medium bowl with electric mixer until soft peaks form; fold into chocolate mixture in two batches. Spread mixture into pan; bake about 15 minutes. Turn cake onto wire rack covered with baking paper; cool to room temperature.
5 Cut out circle of cake large enough to fit 26cm springform tin, using smaller pieces to fit, if necessary. Beat cream in large bowl with electric mixer until slightly thickened. Fold in slightly cooled extra melted chocolate in four batches. Pour mixture over cake base, refrigerate until set.
6 Remove cake from tin, dust with a little extra sifted cocoa, if desired; serve with coffee anglaise.

coffee anglaise Bring milk and beans to the boil in large saucepan; remove from heat, cover, stand 1 hour. Whisk egg yolks and sugar in large bowl, whisk in milk mixture. Return mixture to same pan, stir over heat, without boiling, until slightly thickened, strain; cool to room temperature. Cover, refrigerate until cold.

prep + cook time 1 hour (+ standing, cooling and refrigeration) **serves** 10

double chocolate mousse

100g dark eating chocolate, chopped coarsely
10g unsalted butter, chopped coarsely
1 egg, separated
½ cup (125ml) thickened cream, whipped
1 cup (250ml) thickened cream, whipped, extra
milk chocolate mousse
100g milk eating chocolate, chopped coarsely
10g unsalted butter, chopped coarsely
1 egg, separated
½ cup (125ml) thickened cream, whipped

1 Melt chocolate in small heatproof bowl over small saucepan of
simmering water. Remove from heat; add butter, stir until smooth.
Stir in egg yolk.
2 Beat egg white in small bowl with electric mixer until soft peaks form.
Fold egg white and cream into chocolate mixture, in two batches.
3 Make milk chocolate mousse.
4 Divide dark chocolate mousse among six ¾-cup (180ml) serving
glasses; top with milk chocolate mousse then extra whipped cream.
Cover; refrigerate 3 hours or overnight.
milk chocolate mousse Repeat steps 1 and 2, using milk chocolate in
place of dark chocolate.

prep + cook time 45 minutes (+ refrigeration) **serves** 6

chocolate nut bavarois with raspberry sauce

1 cup (250ml) milk
½ cup (165g) chocolate hazelnut spread
4 egg yolks
¼ cup (55g) caster sugar
2 teaspoons gelatine
1 tablespoon water
300ml thickened cream
raspberry sauce
200g raspberries
2 tablespoons icing sugar

1 Stir milk and chocolate spread in small saucepan over heat until chocolate spread melts; bring to the boil. Transfer to medium bowl.
2 Beat egg yolks and sugar in small bowl with electric mixer until thick and creamy; gradually stir into milk mixture.
3 Sprinkle gelatine over the water in small heatproof jug; stand in small saucepan of simmering water, stirring, until gelatine dissolves. Stir gelatine mixture into warm milk mixture; cool to room temperature.
4 Beat cream in small bowl with electric mixer until soft peaks form; fold into chocolate mixture. Divide bavarois mixture among six ¾-cup (180ml) serving glasses; refrigerate about 4 hours.
5 Make raspberry sauce.
6 Top bavarois with raspberry sauce.
raspberry sauce Push raspberries through sieve into small bowl; discard seeds. Stir in sugar.

prep + cook time 30 minutes (+ refrigeration) **serves** 6

white chocolate mousse

3 eggs, separated
40g butter, chopped
1⅓ cups (200g) white chocolate Melts, melted
300ml thickened cream
2 tablespoons peach schnapps

1 Place egg yolks and butter in medium heatproof bowl, stir over medium saucepan of simmering water until butter is melted. Whisk in chocolate; cool to room temperature.
2 Beat egg whites in medium bowl with electric mixer until soft peaks form. Fold egg whites, whipped cream and schnapps into chocolate mixture, in two batches.
3 Spoon mousse mixture into eight ⅓-cup (80ml) dishes; cover, refrigerate 3 hours or overnight.

prep + cook time 20 minutes (+ cooling and refrigeration) **serves** 8

chocolate mousse puffs

1 cup (250ml) water
80g butter, chopped
1 cup (150g) plain flour
2 tablespoons cocoa powder
4 eggs
drinking chocolate

chocolate mousse filling
125g cream cheese, softened
⅔ cup (150g) caster sugar
2 egg yolks
1⅔ cup (250g) white chocolate
   Melts, melted
600ml thickened cream, whipped

1 Make chocolate mousse filling.
2 Preheat oven to 220°C/200°C fan-forced. Grease oven trays.
3 Bring the water and butter to the boil in medium saucepan, stirring, until butter is melted. Add sifted flour and cocoa all at once, stir vigorously over heat until mixture leaves side of pan and forms a smooth ball.
4 Transfer mixture to small bowl of electric mixer; beat in eggs, one at a time, beating until mixture is thick and glossy between additions.
5 Drop level tablespoons of mixture 4cm apart onto trays; bake about 15 minutes or until pastry is puffed. Using skewer, make a small hole in base of each puff; cool on wire racks.
6 Reduce oven to 200°C/180°C fan-forced
7 Split puffs in half, use a teaspoon to scoop out any uncooked mixture; return halves, cut-side up, to oven trays. Bake about 10 minutes or until puffs are crisp; cool on wire racks.
8 Spoon mousse filling into half of the puffs, replace tops. Serve puffs dusted with sifted drinking chocolate.
chocolate mousse filling Beat cheese, sugar and egg yolks in large bowl with electric mixer until smooth. Just before melted chocolate sets, beat into cheese mixture then fold in cream, in two batches. Cover; refrigerate until cold.

prep + cook time 1 hour (+ refrigeration) **makes** 32
tip Unfilled puffs and chocolate mousse filling can be made a day ahead; assemble just before serving.

chocolate espresso mousse cake

6 eggs, separated
½ cup (80g) icing sugar
¼ cup (25g) cocoa powder
2 tablespoons cornflour
150g dark eating chocolate, melted
1 tablespoon water
1 tablespoon instant coffee granules
1 tablespoon hot water
3 cups (750ml) thickened cream
450g dark eating chocolate, melted, extra
2 teaspoons cocoa powder, extra

1 Preheat oven to 180°C/160°C fan-forced. Grease 25cm x 30cm swiss roll pan; line base and two long sides with baking paper.
2 Beat egg yolks and sugar in small bowl with electric mixer until thick and creamy; transfer mixture to large bowl. Fold in combined sifted cocoa and cornflour, then chocolate and the water.
3 Beat egg whites in small bowl with electric mixer until soft peaks form. Fold egg whites, in two batches, into chocolate mixture. Spread mixture into pan; bake about 15 minutes. Turn cake onto baking-paper-covered wire rack to cool.
4 Grease 23cm springform tin; line side with baking paper, extending paper 5cm above edge of tin. Cut 23cm-diameter circle from cooled cake; place in tin. Discard remaining cake.
5 Dissolve coffee in the hot water in small jug; cool. Beat cream and coffee mixture in medium bowl with electric mixer until soft peaks form. Fold in cooled extra chocolate. Pour mixture over cake in tin, cover; refrigerate about 3 hours or until set.
6 Transfer cake from tin to serving plate; dust with sifted extra cocoa.

prep + cook time 1 hour (+ refrigeration) **serves** 12

milk chocolate rum and raisin mousse

225g milk chocolate Melts, melted
½ cup (120g) sour cream
3 eggs, separated
⅓ cup (55g) finely chopped raisins
1½ tablespoons dark rum
1 tablespoon toasted desiccated coconut
300ml thickened cream, whipped lightly
2 tablespoons caster sugar

1 Combine chocolate, sour cream and egg yolks in large bowl until smooth; stir in raisins, rum and coconut. Fold in cream.
2 Beat egg whites in small bowl with electric mixer until soft peaks form. Gradually beat in sugar until dissolved; fold into chocolate mixture.
3 Spoon mixture into six 1-cup (250ml) serving glasses; decorate with flaked coconut.

prep + cook time 20 minutes **serves** 6
tip This recipe can be made up to 3 days ahead; keep, covered, in refrigerator.

irish cream and dark choc mousse cake

6 eggs, separated
½ cup (80g) icing sugar
¼ cup (25g) cocoa powder
2 tablespoons cornflour
150g dark eating chocolate, melted
1 tablespoon water
600ml thickened cream
450g dark eating chocolate, chopped coarsely, extra
¾ cup (180ml) irish cream liqueur
1 tablespoon cocoa powder, extra

1 Preheat oven to 180°C/160°C fan-forced. Grease 25cm x 30cm swiss roll pan; line base and sides with baking paper.
2 Beat egg yolks and sugar in small bowl with electric mixer until thick and creamy; transfer to large bowl. Fold in combined sifted cocoa and cornflour, then chocolate; fold in the water.
3 Beat egg whites in medium bowl with electric mixer until soft peaks form. Fold egg whites, in two batches, into chocolate mixture. Spread mixture into pan; bake about 15 minutes. Turn cake onto baking-paper-covered wire rack. Cover cake with baking paper; cool to room temperature.
4 Grease 22cm springform tin; line side with baking paper, bringing paper 5cm above edge of tin. Cut 22cm-diameter circle from cooled cake; place in tin. Discard remaining cake.
5 Stir cream and extra chocolate in medium saucepan over low heat until smooth; transfer to large bowl. Refrigerate until just cold.
6 Add liqueur to chocolate mixture; beat with electric mixer until mixture changes to a paler colour. Pour mixture into tin; refrigerate about 3 hours or until set.
7 Transfer cake from tin to serving plate; dust with sifted extra cocoa.

prep + cook time 45 minutes (+ refrigeration) **serves** 12
tip Do not overbeat the chocolate and liqueur mixture as it will curdle.

mocha bavarian with pecan praline

1½ cups (375ml) milk
1 tablespoon instant coffee granules
100g dark eating chocolate, chopped coarsely
4 egg yolks
¾ cup (165g) caster sugar
1 tablespoon gelatine
¼ cup (60g) water
300ml thickened cream, whipped
pecan praline
¼ cup (55g) sugar
1 tablespoon water
½ cup (60g) pecans, chopped coarsely

1 Make pecan praline.
2 Stir milk, coffee and chocolate in small saucepan over low heat, without boiling, until chocolate is melted.
3 Beat egg yolks and sugar in small bowl with electric mixer until thick and pale. With motor operating, gradually add hot milk mixture.
4 Sprinkle gelatine over the water in small heatproof jug; stand jug in small saucepan of simmering water, stir until gelatine dissolves. Stir gelatine mixture into warm chocolate mixture. Refrigerate mixture, stirring occasionally, until just beginning to set.
5 Fold cream and praline into mousse mixture; pour into six ¾-cup (180ml) serving glasses. Refrigerate several hours or until firm.
6 Serve mousse with extra whipped cream, if you like, sprinkled with reserved praline.
pecan praline Stir sugar and the water in small heavy-based saucepan, constantly over heat, without boiling, until sugar dissolves. Bring to the boil; boil rapidly, without stirring, until syrup turns golden brown. Stir in nuts. Pour mixture onto greased oven tray; cool until set. Chop roughly; reserve 2 tablespoons praline for decoration.

prep + cook time 40 minutes (+ refrigeration) **serves** 6
tip This recipe can be made a day ahead; store, covered, in refrigerator.

frozen mocha mousse

dark chocolate layer
100g dark eating chocolate, melted
2 teaspoons coffee-flavoured
   liqueur
2 eggs, separated
½ cup (125ml) thickened cream
milk chocolate layer
100g milk eating chocolate, melted
2 teaspoons coffee-flavoured
   liqueur
2 eggs, separated
½ cup (125ml) thickened cream

white chocolate layer
120g white eating chocolate,
   melted
60g butter, melted
2 teaspoons coffee-flavoured
   liqueur
3 eggs, separated
⅔ cup (120ml) thickened cream

1 Line 14cm x 21cm loaf pan with plastic wrap.
2 To make dark chocolate layer, combine chocolate, liqueur and egg
yolks in large bowl until smooth. Whip cream in small bowl with electric
mixer until soft peaks form; fold into chocolate mixture. Beat egg whites
in small bowl with electric mixer until soft peaks form; fold into chocolate
mixture. Pour mixture into pan; cover with foil, freeze several hours or
until firm.
3 To make milk chocolate layer, combine chocolate, liqueur and egg yolks
in large bowl until smooth. Whip cream in small bowl with electric mixer
until soft peaks form; fold into chocolate mixture. Beat egg whites in
small bowl with electric mixer until soft peaks form; fold into chocolate
mixture. Pour mixture over dark chocolate layer; cover, freeze until firm.
4 To make white chocolate layer, combine chocolate, butter, liqueur
and egg yolks in large bowl until smooth. Whip cream in small bowl
with electric mixer until soft peaks form; fold into chocolate mixture.
Beat egg whites in small bowl with electric mixer until soft peaks form;
fold into chocolate mixture. Pour mixture over milk chocolate layer;
cover, freeze until firm.
5 Turn mousse onto serving plate; remove plastic wrap. Serve mousse
sliced with chocolate sauce, if you like.

prep + cook time 1 hour (+ freezing) **serves** 10
tip This recipe can be made up to a week ahead; store, covered,
in freezer.

marbled mocha mousse

chocolate mousse
200g dark eating chocolate, melted
100g unsalted butter, melted
2 tablespoons coffee-flavoured
  liqueur
4 eggs, beaten lightly
1 tablespoon gelatine
⅓ cup (80ml) water
300ml thickened cream

coffee mousse
200g white eating chocolate,
  melted
100g unsalted butter, melted
2 tablespoons coffee-flavoured
  liqueur
4 eggs, beaten lightly
1 tablespoon instant coffee
  granules
½ cup (125ml) water
1 tablespoon gelatine
1 cup (250ml) thickened cream

1 Line 13.5cm x 23.5cm loaf pan with plastic wrap.
2 To make chocolate mousse, stir chocolate, butter, liqueur and eggs in large bowl until smooth. Sprinkle gelatine over the water in small heatproof jug; stand in small saucepan of simmering water, stirring, until gelatine dissolves. Stir cooled gelatine into chocolate mixture. Beat cream in small bowl with electric mixer until soft peaks form; fold into chocolate mixture. Refrigerate mousse, stirring occasionally, until almost set.
3 To make coffee mousse, stir chocolate, butter, liqueur and eggs in large bowl until smooth. Dissolve coffee in water in small heatproof jug, sprinkle gelatine over coffee; stand in small saucepan of simmering water, stirring, until gelatine dissolves. Stir gelatine mixture into chocolate mixture. Beat cream in small bowl with electric mixer until soft peaks form; fold into chocolate mixture. Refrigerate mousse, stirring occasionally, until almost set.
4 Drop alternating spoonfuls of mousse mixtures into pan. Gently pull a knife or skewer through mixture to create a marbled effect. Cover; refrigerate until set.
5 Turn mousse from pan; remove plastic wrap. Serve mousse sliced.

prep + cook time 1 hour (+ refrigeration) **serves** 10
tip This recipe can be made up to 2 days ahead; store, covered, in refrigerator.

margarita mousse

¼ cup (55g) white sugar
1 tablespoon gelatine
2 tablespoons water
300ml thickened cream
1¼ cups (300g) sour cream
½ cup (120g) spreadable cream cheese
1 cup (220g) caster sugar
green food colouring
¼ cup (60ml) tequila
1 tablespoon cointreau
1 teaspoon finely grated lime rind
¾ cup (180ml) lime juice
⅓ cup (80ml) orange juice

1 Place white sugar on saucer. Dip rims of six ¾-cup (180ml) glasses in bowl of cold water then into white sugar; refrigerate glasses.
2 Sprinkle gelatine over the water in small heatproof jug; stand jug in small saucepan of simmering water. Stir until gelatine dissolves; cool 5 minutes.
3 Beat cream, sour cream, cream cheese and caster sugar in medium bowl with electric mixer until sugar dissolves and mixture is fluffy. Beat in enough colouring to tint mixture a pale green. Whisk tequila, liqueur, rind, juices and gelatine mixture into cream mixture.
4 Divide mixture among glasses; refrigerate about 2 hours or until mousse sets.

prep + cook time 25 minutes (+ refrigeration) **serves** 6
tip This recipe can be made a day ahead; store, covered, in refrigerator.

fresh raspberry mousse

500g fresh raspberries
2 egg yolks
⅓ cup (75g) caster sugar
2 teaspoons gelatine
2 tablespoons water
1 cup (250ml) thickened cream

1 Push half the berries through a sieve; discard seeds.
2 Beat egg yolks and sugar in small bowl with electric mixer until pale and thick; fold in raspberry puree. Sprinkle gelatine over the water in small heatproof jug; stand jug in small saucepan of simmering water, stirring, until gelatine dissolves. Cool 5 minutes; stir into berry mixture.
3 Beat cream in small bowl with electric mixer until soft peaks form; fold into berry mixture.
4 Pour mixture into four 1-cup (250ml) dessert glasses; refrigerate 3 hours or until set. Serve with remaining raspberries and whipped cream, if you like.

prep + cook time 20 minutes (+ refrigeration) **serves** 4
tip Frozen raspberries can be substituted for fresh, but they should be thawed before using.

berry mousse cake

4 egg whites
¾ cup (165g) caster sugar
1½ cups (240g) almond meal
¼ cup (35g) plain flour
300ml thickened cream
450g fresh raspberries
½ cup (160g) raspberry jam,
  warmed
¼ cup (60ml) coconut-flavoured
  liqueur

raspberry mousse
200g fresh raspberries
3 teaspoons gelatine
2 tablespoons water
125g white eating chocolate,
  melted
2 egg yolks
¼ cup (55g) caster sugar
1 tablespoon coconut-flavoured
  liqueur
300ml thickened cream

1 Preheat oven to 180°C/160°C fan-forced. Grease two 22cm springform tins; line bases with baking paper.
2 Beat egg whites in medium bowl with electric mixer until soft peaks form. Gradually add sugar, beating between additions, until sugar dissolves; fold in dry ingredients. Spread mixture equally between tins.
3 Bake cakes about 20 minutes. Stand cakes 5 minutes. Remove from tins; cool at room temperature.
4 Meanwhile, make raspberry mousse.
5 Line base and side of clean 22cm springform tin with baking paper; place one cake into tin. Pour raspberry mousse over cake; top with remaining cake. Cover; refrigerate 3 hours or overnight, until mousse sets.
6 Remove cake from tin. Beat cream in small bowl with electric mixer until soft peaks form; spread all over cake. Place raspberries on top of cake; brush raspberries with combined strained jam and liqueur.
raspberry mousse Push raspberries through sieve into large bowl; discard seeds. Sprinkle gelatine over the water in small heatproof jug. Stand jug in small saucepan of simmering water; stir until gelatine dissolves. Combine gelatine mixture, chocolate, egg yolks, sugar and liqueur in small bowl; stir until smooth. Beat cream in small bowl with electric mixer until soft peaks form; fold cream and chocolate mixture into raspberry puree.

prep + cook time 1 hour (+ refrigeration) **serves** 12
tips The cake, without the topping, can be made a day ahead. If you don't like the taste of coconut in your liqueur, use plain white rum instead.

berry mousse

2 teaspoons gelatine
2 tablespoons water
2 egg whites
⅓ cup (75g) caster sugar
400g low-fat berry-flavoured yogurt
150g fresh mixed berries

1 Sprinkle gelatine over the water in small heatproof jug; place jug in small pan of simmering water, stir until gelatine dissolves. Cool.
2 Meanwhile, beat egg whites in small bowl with electric mixer until soft peaks form. Gradually add sugar, beating until sugar dissolves.
3 Place yogurt in medium bowl; stir in gelatine mixture, then fold in egg-white mixture.
4 Spoon mousse mixture into serving bowl, cover; refrigerate about 2 hours or until set. Serve mousse topped with mixed berries.

prep + cook time 10 minutes (+ refrigeration) **serves** 4

honey mousse

40g butter
5 eggs, separated
¾ cup (135g) white chocolate Melts
¼ cup (60ml) honey
2 teaspoons gelatine
2 tablespoons water
300ml thickened cream

1 Grease six 1-cup (250ml) dishes.
2 Stir butter, egg yolks, chocolate and honey in medium saucepan over heat, without boiling, until chocolate is melted. Transfer mixture to large bowl.
3 Sprinkle gelatine over water in jug; stand jug in small saucepan of simmering water, stirring until gelatine dissolves. Stir gelatine mixture into chocolate mixture; cover, cool to room temperature.
4 Beat cream in small bowl with electric mixer until soft peaks form; fold into chocolate mixture. Beat egg whites in small bowl with electric mixer until soft peaks form; fold into chocolate mixture, in two batches.
5 Spoon mixture into dishes; refrigerate 3 hours or overnight.

prep + cook time 20 minutes (+ cooling and refrigeration) **serves** 6

honey lime bavarois

1 cup (250ml) buttermilk
6 egg yolks
¾ cup (165g) caster sugar
2 tablespoons honey
1 tablespoon finely grated
  lime rind
1 tablespoon lime juice
3 teaspoons gelatine
1 tablespoon water
1 egg white
300ml thickened cream

syrup
1 cup (220g) caster sugar
⅔ cup (160ml) water
1 tablespoon finely grated
  lime rind
½ cup (125ml) apple juice
⅓ cup (80ml) lime juice
1 ½ tablespoons gin

1 Grease six ½-cup (125ml) moulds.
2 Whisk buttermilk, egg yolks, sugar and honey in medium saucepan, stirring over heat, without boiling, until custard thickens slightly. Stir in rind and juice; transfer to large bowl.
3 Sprinkle gelatine over water in jug; stand jug in small saucepan simmering water, stir until gelatine dissolves; cool 5 minutes. Stir gelatine mixture into custard; cover surface with plastic wrap, refrigerate about 1 hour or until mixture is the consistency of unbeaten egg white.
4 Beat egg white in small bowl with electric mixer until soft peaks form. Beat cream in medium bowl with electric mixer until soft peaks form; fold into custard mixture, in two batches. Fold in egg white.
5 Spoon mixture into moulds; refrigerate about 3 hours or until set.
6 Make syrup.
7 Turn bavarois onto serving plates, serve with syrup.
syrup Stir sugar, the water, rind and juices in small saucepan over heat, without boiling, until sugar dissolves. Simmer, uncovered, without stirring, about 15 minutes or until mixture thickens. Stir in gin.

prep + cook time 30 minutes (+ refrigeration) **serves** 6
tip You will need about 8 limes for this recipe.

mango creams

2 cups chopped fresh mango
2 tablespoons cointreau
½ cup (125ml) orange juice
1 tablespoon gelatine
½ cup (125ml) water
½ cup (125ml) thickened cream
2 egg whites
1 tablespoon caster sugar

1 Grease ten ½-cup (125ml) moulds.
2 Blend or process mango, liqueur and juice until smooth; transfer to large bowl.
3 Sprinkle gelatine over water in jug; stand jug in small saucepan simmering water, stir until gelatine dissolves; cool 5 minutes. Stir gelatine mixture into mango mixture.
4 Beat cream in small bowl with electric mixer until soft peaks form; fold cream into mango mixture. Beat egg whites in small bowl with electric mixer until soft peaks form; beat in sugar until sugar is dissolved. Fold egg white mixture into mango mixture.
5 Pour mixture into moulds; refrigerate until set. Turn onto plates, serve with extra cream and roasted flaked almonds, if you like.

prep + cook time 30 minutes (+ refrigeration) **serves** 10
tip You will need about 2 large mangoes (900g) for this recipe.

glacé ginger and peach mousse

3 eggs, separated
¼ cup (55g) caster sugar
1½ cups (375ml) milk
1 tablespoon gelatine
¼ cup (60ml) water
300ml thickened cream
¼ cup (55g) chopped
   glacé ginger
¼ cup (60g) chopped
   glacé peaches

ginger sauce
1 cup (250ml) water
½ cup (175g) golden syrup
¼ cup (55g) chopped
   glacé ginger
2 teaspoons cornflour
2 teaspoons water, extra

1 Grease 1.25-litre (5-cup) ring mould.
2 Beat egg yolks and sugar in small bowl with electric mixer until thick and creamy. Heat milk in medium saucepan until lukewarm; beat into egg mixture while motor is operating. Return mixture to pan; stir over heat, without boiling, until mixture is slightly thickened. Transfer to large bowl.
3 Sprinkle gelatine over water in small jug; stand jug in small saucepan of simmering water, stir until dissolved. Stir gelatine mixture into egg mixture, cool to room temperature; do not allow to set.
4 Beat cream in small bowl with electric mixer until soft peaks form; stir in ginger and peaches. Fold cream mixture into egg mixture.
5 Beat egg whites in small bowl with electric mixer until firm peaks form; fold into egg mixture. Pour into mould; refrigerate until set.
6 Make ginger sauce.
7 Turn mousse onto serving plate, sprinkle with extra peaches, if you like, and serve with sauce.
ginger sauce Blend or process the water, golden syrup and ginger until smooth, pour into small saucepan. Blend cornflour with extra water; stir into ginger mixture, over high heat until mixture boils and thickens slightly. Cool before serving.

prep + cook time 30 minutes (+ cooling and refrigeration) **serves** 8

piña colada mousse

1 cup (240g) drained crushed pineapple
3 teaspoons gelatine
¼ cup (60ml) water
3 eggs, separated
½ cup (110g) caster sugar
⅓ cup (80ml) coconut cream
⅓ cup (80ml) pineapple juice
2 tablespoons white rum
⅔ cup (160ml) thickened cream

1 Spoon pineapple into four 1 cup (250ml) glasses.
2 Sprinkle gelatine over water in small jug; stand jug in small saucepan of simmering water, stir until dissolved. Cool to room temperature; do not allow to set.
3 Beat egg yolks and sugar in small bowl with electric mixer until thick and creamy. Stir in coconut cream, juice, rum and gelatine mixture; transfer to large bowl.
4 Beat cream in small bowl with electric mixer until soft peaks from; fold into coconut cream mixture. Beat egg whites in small bowl with electric mixer until soft peaks form; fold into coconut mixture.
5 Pour mixture into glasses; refrigerate until set. Decorate with whipped cream and toasted shredded coconut, if you like.

prep + cook time 20 minutes (+ refrigeration) **serves** 4

spicy pumpkin and hazelnut mousse

2½ teaspoons gelatine
⅓ cup (80ml) water
½ cup (110g) caster sugar
2 teaspoons grated lemon rind
¼ cup (30g) finely chopped, roasted hazelnuts
½ teaspoon ground nutmeg
½ teaspoon ground ginger
1 cup cooked mashed pumpkin
⅓ cup (80ml) lemon juice
4 egg whites

1 Sprinkle gelatine over water in small jug; stand jug in small saucepan of simmering water, stir until dissolved; cool.
2 Blend or process sugar, rind, nuts, spices, pumpkin, juice and gelatine mixture until smooth; transfer to large bowl.
3 Beat egg whites in small bowl with electric mixer until soft peaks form; fold into pumpkin mixture.
4 Pour mousse into six ¾-cup (180ml) dishes; refrigerate until firm.
Serve topped with whipped cream and ground hazelnuts, if you like.

prep + cook time 20 minutes (+ refrigeration) **serves** 6
tip You will need to cook about 350g pumpkin for this recipe.

rockmelon passionfruit mousse

4 cups (750g) chopped rockmelon
2 tablespoons honey
200g plain yogurt
1 tablespoon gelatine
2 tablespoons water
2 tablespoons passionfruit pulp

1 Blend or process rockmelon, honey and yogurt until smooth; transfer to large bowl.
2 Sprinkle gelatine over water in small jug; stand jug in small saucepan of simmering water, stir until dissolved. Stir gelatine mixture and passionfruit pulp into melon mixture.
3 Pour mousse into six ¾-cup (180ml) serving dishes; refrigerate several hours or until set.

prep + cook time 20 minutes (+ refrigeration) **serves** 6
tip You will need 1kg rockmelon and about 2 passionfruit for this recipe.

fluffy fruit mousse

⅔ cup (160ml) apricot nectar
⅔ cup (160ml) pear juice
2 teaspoons gelatine
2 tablespoons water
2 teaspoons caster sugar
1 egg, separated
1 medium fresh or canned peach (150g), sliced

1 Pour juices into separate small bowls.
2 Sprinkle gelatine over water in small jug; stand jug in small saucepan of simmering water, stir until dissolved. Cool to room temperature.
3 Combine sugar and egg yolk in small bowl; stir in gelatine mixture. Divide mixture evenly between bowls of fruit juices; refrigerate fruit mixtures until set to the consistency of unbeaten egg white.
4 Beat egg white in small bowl with electric mixer until soft peaks form; fold half into each bowl of fruit mixture.
5 Pour mixtures simultaneously into four ½ cup (125ml) dishes; refrigerate until set. Decorate with peach slices.

prep + cook time 25 minutes (+ refrigeration) **serves** 4

mango and lime mousse

3 eggs, separated
½ cup (110g) caster sugar
2 teaspoons gelatine
1 tablespoon water
⅓ cup (80ml) lime or lemon juice
¼ cup (60ml) dry white wine
2 teaspoons crème de menthe
850g can mango slices, drained
1 cup (250ml) thickened cream

1 Beat egg yolks and sugar in medium heatproof bowl until light and creamy. Place bowl over medium saucepan of simmering water, ensuring that the water doesn't touch the bottom of the bowl. Stir until sugar dissolves and mixture is thick.
2 Sprinkle gelatine over water in small jug; stand jug in small saucepan of simmering water, stir until dissolved. Stir gelatine mixture into egg yolk mixture; remove from heat. Stir in juice, wine and crème de menthe; cool. Stir in mashed mangoes.
3 Beat cream in small bowl with electric mixer until soft peaks from; fold into mango mixture. Beat egg whites in small bowl with electric mixer until soft peaks form; fold into mango mixture.
4 Spoon mousse into eight ¾ cup (180ml) dishes or 1.75-litre (7-cup) serving dish; refrigerate until set. Serve with extra whipped cream and slices of lime or lemon.

prep + cook time 20 minutes (+ refrigeration) **serves** 8

chocolate zabaglione

4 egg yolks
1/3 cup (75g) caster sugar
1/3 cup (80ml) marsala
3 teaspoons cocoa powder

1 Combine egg yolks and sugar in medium heatproof bowl. Place bowl over medium saucepan of simmering water, ensuring that the water doesn't touch bottom of bowl. Beat with electric mixer until thick and creamy.
2 Gradually beat in combined marsala and sifted cocoa, beating constantly, further 5 minutes or until mixture is thick and creamy.
3 Spoon mixture into four 2/3 cup (160ml) serving glasses.

prep + cook time 15 minutes **serves** 4
tip Zabaglione should be made just before serving.

SELF-SAUCING
PUDDINGS

chocolate, pear and hazelnut self-saucing pudding

100g dark eating chocolate,
  chopped coarsely
50g butter
⅔ cup (160ml) milk
¼ cup (25g) ground hazelnuts
⅔ cup (100g) roasted hazelnuts,
  chopped coarsely
1 cup (220g) firmly packed
  brown sugar
1 cup (150g) self-raising flour
1 egg, beaten lightly

2 medium pears (460g)
300ml thickened cream
2 tablespoons icing sugar
2 tablespoons hazelnut-flavoured
  liqueur
fudge sauce
1¾ cups (430ml) water
100g butter
1 cup (220g) firmly packed
  brown sugar
½ cup (50g) cocoa powder, sifted

1 Preheat oven to 180°C/160°C fan-forced. Grease shallow 3 litre (12 cup) baking dish.

2 Stir chocolate, butter and milk in small saucepan over low heat until smooth. Transfer to large bowl; stir in ground hazelnut, nuts and brown brown sugar then flour and egg.

3 Peel and core pears; slice thinly. Place pear slices, slightly overlapping, in dish; top with chocolate mixture.

4 Make fudge sauce; pour over chocolate mixture.

5 Bake pudding about 1 hour. Stand 10 minutes.

6 Meanwhile, beat cream, icing sugar and liqueur in small bowl with electric mixer until soft peaks form.

7 Serve pudding warm, topped with liqueur cream.

fudge sauce Stir ingredients in small saucepan over low heat until smooth.

prep + cook time 1 hour 30 minutes (+ standing) **serves** 6
tips We used Frangelico for the hazelnut-flavoured liqueur – it can be omitted from the whipped cream mixture for an alcohol-free dessert.

lemon delicious pudding

125g butter, melted
2 teaspoons finely grated lemon rind
1½ cups (330g) caster sugar
3 eggs, separated
½ cup (75g) self-raising flour
⅓ cup (80ml) lemon juice
1⅓ cups (330ml) milk

1 Preheat oven to 180°C/160°C fan-forced. Grease six 1 cup (250ml) ovenproof dishes.
2 Combine butter, rind, sugar and yolks in large bowl. Stir in sifted flour then juice. Gradually stir in milk; mixture should be smooth and runny.
3 Beat egg whites in small bowl with electric mixer until soft peaks form; fold into lemon mixture, in two batches.
4 Place ovenproof dishes in large baking dish; divide lemon mixture among dishes. Add enough boiling water to baking dish to come halfway up sides of ovenproof dishes.
5 Bake pudding about 45 minutes.

prep + cook time 1 hour **serves** 6

lemon and mixed berry self-saucing pudding

¾ cup (110g) self-raising flour
½ cup (110g) caster sugar
½ cup (125ml) skim milk
1 tablespoon finely grated lemon rind
30g unsalted butter, melted
⅓ cup (55g) icing sugar
⅔ cup (160ml) boiling water
mixed berry sauce
1 cup (150g) frozen mixed berries
1 tablespoon caster sugar
1 tablespoon water

1 Grease four deep 1¼ cup (310ml) microwave-proof dishes.
2 Make mixed berry sauce.
3 Sift flour into medium bowl. Add sugar, milk, rind and butter; whisk until batter is smooth.
4 Divide berry sauce among dishes then top with batter; dust with sifted icing sugar. Pour the boiling water over puddings. Microwave, uncovered, on MEDIUM (55%) about 10 minutes.
mixed berry sauce Bring ingredients to the boil in small saucepan. Boil, uncovered, 1 minute. Remove from heat.

prep + cook time 20 minutes **serves** 4

jaffa self-saucing pudding

60g butter
½ cup (125ml) milk
½ teaspoon vanilla extract
¾ cup (165g) caster sugar
½ cup (90g) rice flour
⅓ cup (40g) soya flour
⅓ cup (45g) gluten-free self-raising flour
1 teaspoon gluten-free baking powder
2 tablespoons cocoa powder
2 teaspoons finely grated orange rind
½ cup (110g) firmly packed brown sugar
2 cups (500ml) boiling water

1 Preheat oven to 180°C/160°C fan-forced. Grease 1.5 litre (6 cup) ovenproof dish.
2 Melt butter with milk and extract in medium saucepan. Remove from heat; whisk in caster sugar, then sifted flours, baking powder, half the cocoa and rind. Spread mixture into dish.
3 Sift brown sugar and the remaining cocoa over mixture; gently pour the boiling water over mixture.
4 Bake pudding about 40 minutes. Stand 5 minutes before serving.

prep + cook time 1 hour **serves** 6
tips This recipe is gluten-free, wheat-free, yeast-free, egg-free and nut-free. This pudding can be stored in an airtight container in the refrigerator for up to 2 days.

chocolate self-saucing pudding

60g butter
½ cup (125ml) milk
½ teaspoon vanilla extract
¾ cup (165g) caster sugar
1 cup (150g) self-raising flour
1 tablespoon cocoa powder
¾ cup (165g) firmly packed brown sugar
1 tablespoon cocoa powder, extra
2 cups (500ml) boiling water

1 Preheat oven to 180°C/160°C fan-forced. Grease 1.5 litre (6 cup) ovenproof dish.
2 Melt butter with milk in medium saucepan. Remove from heat; stir in extract and caster sugar then sifted flour and cocoa. Spread mixture into dish. Sift brown sugar and extra cocoa over mixture; gently pour the boiling water over mixture.
3 Bake pudding about 40 minutes or until centre is firm. Stand 5 minutes before serving.

prep + cook time 50 minutes (+ standing) **serves** 6

date and butterscotch self-saucing pudding

1 cup (150g) self-raising flour
½ cup (110g) firmly packed brown sugar
20g butter, melted
½ cup (125ml) milk
½ cup (70g) finely chopped dried seedless dates
caramel sauce
½ cup (110g) firmly packed brown sugar
1¾ cups (430ml) boiling water
50g butter

1 Preheat oven to 180°C/160°C fan-forced. Grease 2 litre (8 cup) shallow ovenproof dish.
2 Combine flour, sugar, butter, milk and dates in medium bowl. Spread mixture into dish.
3 Make caramel sauce; pour sauce slowly over back of spoon onto mixture in dish.
4 Bake pudding about 45 minutes or until centre is firm. Stand 5 minutes before serving.
caramel sauce Stir ingredients in medium heatproof jug until sugar is dissolved.

prep + cook time 1 hour **serves** 6

mocha, pear and nut self-saucing pudding

100g dark eating chocolate, chopped
150g butter
⅔ cup (160ml) milk
1½ tablespoons instant coffee granules
⅔ cup (70g) ground hazelnuts
¾ cup (165g) firmly packed brown sugar
1 cup (150g) self-raising flour
1 egg
2 medium pears (460g), sliced thinly
1¾ cups (430ml) water
¾ cup (165g) firmly packed brown sugar, extra
½ cup (50g) cocoa powder

1 Preheat oven to 180°C/160°C fan-forced. Grease eight 1¼ cup (310ml) ovenproof dishes or a shallow 2.5 litre (10 cup) ovenproof dish.
2 Stir chocolate, 50g of the butter, milk and coffee in small saucepan over low heat until smooth. Transfer to large bowl; stir in ground hazelnuts, sugar, then sifted flour and egg.
3 Place pear slices, slightly overlapping, in dishes; top with chocolate mixture.
4 Stir the water, extra sugar, sifted cocoa and remaining butter in small saucepan over low heat until smooth; pour over chocolate mixture.
5 Bake pudding about 30 minutes (or about 45 minutes for larger pudding). Stand 5 minutes before serving.

prep + cook time 1 hour (+ standing) **serves** 8

microwave choc-cherry self-saucing pudding

60g butter, chopped
1½ cups (225g) self-raising flour
1 cup (220g) caster sugar
⅓ cup (35g) cocoa powder
1¼ cups (310ml) milk
1 teaspoon vanilla extract
2 x 55g Cherry Ripe bars, chopped coarsely
½ cup (110g) firmly packed brown sugar
1 tablespoon cocoa powder, extra
2 cups (500ml) boiling water
50g butter, chopped, extra

1 Melt butter in deep 3 litre (12 cup) microwave-safe dish, uncovered, on HIGH (100%) in microwave oven about 1 minute or until butter has melted. Using oven mitts, remove dish from microwave oven.
2 Add sifted flour, caster sugar and cocoa to dish with milk and extract; whisk until smooth. Stir in Cherry Ripe.
3 Combine brown sugar and sifted extra cocoa in medium jug; gradually stir in the boiling water. Add extra butter; stir until butter melts. Carefully pour syrup mixture evenly over pudding mixture.
4 Cook, uncovered, on HIGH (100%) in microwave oven about 15 minutes or until just cooked in centre. Remove dish from microwave oven; stand 5 minutes before serving with cream.

prep + cook time 25 minutes **serves** 8

chocolate hazelnut self-saucing puddings

½ cup (125ml) milk
40g dark eating chocolate,
  chopped coarsely
50g butter
⅓ cup (35g) cocoa powder
½ cup (75g) self-raising flour
¼ cup (25g) ground hazelnuts
⅓ cup (75g) caster sugar
⅔ cup (150g) firmly packed
  brown sugar
1 egg, beaten lightly
¾ cup (180ml) water
40g butter, chopped, extra
200g vanilla ice-cream

chocolate hazelnut sauce
½ cup (125ml) cream
2 tablespoons brown sugar
50g dark eating chocolate,
  chopped finely
⅓ cup (110g) chocolate
  hazelnut spread
1 tablespoon hazelnut-flavoured
  liqueur

1 Preheat oven to 180°C/160°C fan-forced. Grease four 1 cup (250ml) ovenproof dishes.
2 Stir milk, chocolate, butter and half of the cocoa in small saucepan over low heat until smooth.
3 Combine flour, ground hazelnuts, caster sugar and half of the brown sugar in medium bowl. Add chocolate mixture and egg; stir until combined. Divide mixture among dishes.
4 Stir the water, extra butter, remaining brown sugar and remaining cocoa in small saucepan over low heat until smooth. Pour hot mixture gently and evenly over puddings.
5 Bake puddings about 25 minutes. Stand 5 minutes.
6 Meanwhile, make chocolate hazelnut sauce.
7 Serve puddings topped with ice-cream then sauce.
chocolate hazelnut sauce Bring cream and sugar to the boil in small saucepan. Remove from heat, add chocolate; stir until smooth. Stir in spread and liqueur until smooth.

prep + cook time 40 minutes **serves** 4
tips We used Frangelico for the hazelnut-flavoured liqueur. This dessert is best served hot because the sauce is quickly absorbed by the puddings.

pineapple self-saucing pudding

30g butter
2 teaspoons grated lemon rind
½ cup (110g) caster sugar
3 eggs, separated
2 tablespoons self-raising flour
1 cup (250ml) milk
½ cup (40g) desiccated coconut
450g can crushed pineapple, drained

1 Preheat oven to 180°C/160°C fan-forced. Grease 1 litre (4 cup) ovenproof dish.
2 Beat butter, rind, sugar and egg yolks in small bowl with electric mixer until thick and creamy; transfer to large bowl. Stir in sifted flour, milk and coconut, in two batches. Stir in pineapple.
3 Beat egg whites in small bowl with electric mixer until soft peaks form; fold into pineapple mixture. Pour mixture into dish.
4 Bake pudding about 40 minutes or until firm. Stand 5 minutes before serving. Dust with sifted icing sugar.

prep + cook time 1 hour (+ standing) **serves** 6

ginger and orange self-saucing pudding

90g butter
2 teaspoons grated orange rind
⅓ cup (75g) brown sugar
¼ cup (90g) golden syrup
1 egg
1 tablespoon chopped glacé ginger
1 cup (150g) self-raising flour
2 teaspoons ground ginger
½ cup (125ml) milk
¼ cup (55g) caster sugar
1 teaspoon cornflour
1 cup (250ml) green ginger wine

1 Preheat oven to 180°C/160°C fan-forced. Grease 1 litre (4 cup) ovenproof dish.
2 Beat butter, rind, brown sugar and golden syrup in small bowl with electric mixer until light and fluffy; beat in egg. Stir in glacé ginger, sifted flour and ground ginger with milk, in two batches. Pour mixture into dish.
3 Blend caster sugar and cornflour with 1 tablespoon of the wine in small saucepan; stir in remaining wine. Stir over high heat until mixture boils; pour gently over pudding mixture in dish.
4 Bake pudding about 50 minutes or until firm. Stand 5 minutes before serving. Dust with sifted icing sugar.

prep + cook time 1 hour 10 minutes (+ standing) **serves** 6

hazelnut butterscotch self-saucing pudding

¾ cup (110g) self-raising flour
¼ cup (25g) ground hazelnuts
390g sweetened condensed milk
30g butter
1 teaspoon vanilla extract
½ cup (125ml) milk
¾ cup (165g) firmly packed brown sugar
1¼ cups (310ml) boiling water

1 Preheat oven to 180°C/160°C fan-forced. Grease 2 litre (8 cup) ovenproof dish.
2 Sift flour into medium bowl; stir in ground hazelnuts.
3 Stir condensed milk in small heavy-based saucepan over medium heat about 10 minutes or until thickened slightly and pale golden brown. Stir in butter, extract and milk until butter is melted; stand until warm. Pour milk mixture into flour mixture; mix well.
4 Pour mixture into dish; sift brown sugar onto pudding mixture, carefully pour water evenly over top of pudding.
5 Bake pudding about 35 minutes or until firm. Stand 5 minutes before serving. Dust with sifted icing sugar.

prep + cook time 1 hour (+ standing) **serves** 6

orange and raspberry self-saucing pudding

¼ cup (20g) flaked almonds
30g butter
¾ cup (110g) self-raising flour
⅓ cup (80ml) milk
⅔ cup (150g) firmly packed brown sugar
2 teaspoons finely grated orange rind
¾ cup (110g) frozen raspberries
¼ cup (60ml) orange juice
¾ cup (180ml) boiling water

1 Grease shallow 1.5 litre (6 cup) microwave-safe dish.
2 Place nuts in small microwave-safe bowl; cook, uncovered, in microwave oven on HIGH (100%) about 2 minutes or until browned lightly.
3 Place butter in medium microwave-safe bowl; cook, uncovered, in microwave oven on HIGH (100%) 30 seconds. Add flour, milk and half of the sugar; whisk until smooth. Stir in rind and raspberries; spread into dish.
4 Sprinkle remaining sugar over raspberry mixture; carefully pour over combined juice and the boiling water.
5 Place pudding on microwave-safe rack; cook, uncovered, in microwave oven on MEDIUM-HIGH (70%-80%) about 12 minutes. Stand 5 minutes. Sprinkle pudding with nuts. Serve with cream or ice-cream.

prep + cook time 20 minutes (+ standing) **serves** 4
tips If cooking in a conventional oven, grease 1.5 litre (6 cup) ovenproof dish. Bake, uncovered, in 200°C/180°C fan-forced oven about 20 minutes. This recipe is best made close to serving.

SOUFFLES

chocolate soufflé

⅓ cup (75g) caster sugar
50g butter
1 tablespoon plain flour
200g dark eating chocolate, melted
2 egg yolks
4 egg whites

1 Preheat oven to 180°C/160°C fan-forced. Grease four ¾ cup (180ml) soufflé dishes. Sprinkle inside of dishes with a little of the sugar; shake away excess. Place dishes on oven tray.
2 Melt butter in small saucepan, add flour; cook, stirring, about 2 minutes or until mixture thickens and bubbles. Remove from heat; stir in chocolate and egg yolks. Transfer to large bowl.
3 Beat egg whites in small bowl with electric mixer until soft peaks form. Gradually add remaining sugar, beating until sugar dissolves. Fold egg white mixture into chocolate mixture, in two batches. Divide mixture among dishes.
4 Bake soufflés 15 minutes. Serve immediately, dusted with cocoa powder.

prep + cook time 40 minutes **serves** 4
tip Soufflés must be made just before serving.

hot chocolate soufflés with liqueur cream

2 tablespoons caster sugar
1 tablespoon cornflour
1 tablespoon plain flour
½ cup (110g) caster sugar, extra
½ cup (125ml) milk
⅓ cup (35g) cocoa powder
1 tablespoon instant coffee granules
4 eggs, separated
2 egg whites
liqueur cream
1½ cups (375g) mascarpone cheese
2 tablespoons icing sugar
¼ cup (60ml) coffee-flavoured liqueur

1 Make liqueur cream.
2 Preheat oven to 200°C/180°C fan-forced. Grease eight ¾ cup (180ml) ovenproof dishes. Sprinkle base and sides with sugar; shake away excess sugar. Place dishes on oven tray.
3 Blend flours and extra sugar with some of the milk in small saucepan, whisk in remaining milk, whisk over heat until mixture boils and thickens; remove from heat. Whisk in combined cocoa and coffee until dissolved. Whisk in egg yolks; transfer mixture to large bowl.
4 Beat egg whites in small bowl with electric mixer until firm peaks form; fold about one-quarter of the egg whites into chocolate mixture, then fold in remaining whites. Spoon mixture into dishes.
5 Bake soufflés about 20 minutes or until puffed. Serve immediately, with liqueur cream, sprinkled with a little sifted cocoa powder.
liqueur cream Beat ingredients in small bowl with electric mixer until just combined.

prep + cook time 40 minutes **serves** 8
tips Soufflés must be made just before serving. Liqueur cream can be made a day ahead; refrigerate until required.

frozen chocolate and coconut soufflés

¼ cup (25g) cocoa powder
2 teaspoons plain flour
⅓ cup (75g) caster sugar
¾ cup (180ml) milk
2 eggs, separated
60g white eating chocolate, melted
200ml coconut cream
2 tablespoons caster sugar, extra
300ml thickened cream

1 Place collar of foil around each of six ½ cup (125ml) dishes;
secure with string.
2 Combine sifted cocoa and flour with sugar in small saucepan;
gradually stir in milk. Stir constantly over heat until mixture boils and
thickens slightly. Remove from heat; quickly stir in lightly beaten egg
yolks. Transfer mixture to medium bowl, cover with plastic wrap; cool
to room temperature.
3 Combine white chocolate and coconut cream in large bowl.
4 Beat egg whites in small bowl with electric mixer until soft peaks
form; beat in extra sugar, a tablespoon as a time, until dissolved.
Beat cream in small bowl with electric mixer until soft peaks form.
5 Gently fold half the egg white mixture and half the cream into cocoa
mixture, then fold the remaining egg white mixture and cream into white
chocolate mixture. Drop teaspoonsfuls of both mixtures into each dish.
Using a skewer, swirl through mixtures for a marbled effect.
6 Freeze soufflés for several hours or until just firm. Remove collars,
serve with extra whipped cream.

prep + cook time 40 minutes (+ freezing) **serves** 6
tips These soufflés can be made up to 3 days ahead; keep, covered,
in freezer. Stand at room temperature 10 minutes before serving.

chocolate liqueur soufflés

1 tablespoon caster sugar
1½ cups (375ml) milk
2 tablespoons chocolate-flavoured liqueur
125g dark eating chocolate, chopped
60g butter
¼ cup (35g) plain flour
¼ cup (55g) caster sugar, extra
4 eggs, separated
2 egg whites, extra
2 teaspoons icing sugar

1 Preheat oven to 200°C/180°C fan-forced. Grease four 1 cup (250ml) ovenproof dishes. Sprinkle base and sides with sugar; shake away excess sugar. Place dishes on oven tray.
2 Stir milk, liqueur and chocolate in medium saucepan over low heat until chocolate melts.
3 Melt butter in separate medium saucepan; stir in flour over medium heat for 1 minute. Remove from heat; gradually stir in chocolate mixture and extra sugar, stir over high heat until mixture boils and thickens. Transfer to large bowl; stir in egg yolks
4 Beat all egg whites in large bowl with electric mixer until soft peaks form; fold into chocolate mixture, in two batches. Spoon mixture into dishes.
5 Bake soufflés about 25 minutes or until puffed and well browned. Serve immediately, dusted with sifted icing sugar.

prep + cook time 45 minutes **serves** 4
tips We used crème de cacao, but you could use any chocolate-flavoured liqueur you like. Soufflés must be made just before serving.

passionfruit soufflés

1 tablespoon caster sugar
2 egg yolks
⅓ cup (80ml) passionfruit pulp
2 tablespoons orange-flavoured liqueur
½ cup (80g) icing sugar
4 egg whites
2 teaspoons icing sugar, extra

1 Preheat oven to 200°C/180°C fan-forced. Grease four 1 cup (250ml) soufflé dishes; sprinkle bases and sides with caster sugar, shake away excess. Place dishes on oven tray.
2 Whisk yolks, passionfruit pulp, liqueur and 2 tablespoons of the icing sugar in large bowl until mixture is combined.
3 Beat egg whites in small bowl with electric mixer until soft peaks form. Gradually add remaining icing sugar; beat until firm peaks form. Fold egg white mixture into passionfruit mixture, in two batches. Spoon mixture into dishes.
4 Bake soufflés about 12 minutes or until puffed and browned lightly. Serve immediately, dusted with extra sifted icing sugar.

prep + cook time 30 minutes **serves** 4
tips You will need about 4 passionfruit for this recipe. Soufflés must be made just before serving.

black forest soufflés

1½ tablespoons caster sugar
50g butter
1 tablespoon cocoa powder
½ cup (125ml) buttermilk
125g dark eating chocolate,
  chopped
¼ cup (55g) caster sugar, extra
2 egg yolks
4 egg whites

cherry filling
400g cherries, seeded, halved
⅓ cup (75g) caster sugar
2 tablespoons kirsch
1 tablespoon lemon juice

1 Preheat oven to 220°C/200°C fan-forced. Grease six ¾ cup (180ml) soufflé dishes. Sprinkle inside of dishes with sugar; shake away excess. Place dishes on oven tray.
2 Make cherry filling.
3 Meanwhile, melt butter in small saucepan, stir in cocoa until smooth. Stir in buttermilk, heat without boiling. Remove from heat; stir in chocolate and half of the extra sugar until smooth. Transfer mixture to large bowl; stir in egg yolks.
4 Beat egg whites in small bowl with electric mixer until soft peaks form; beat in remaining extra sugar until dissolved. Fold egg white mixture into chocolate mixture, in two batches.
5 Divide cherry mixture among dishes, then top with chocolate mixture.
6 Bake soufflés 12 minutes or until lightly puffed. Serve immediately.
cherry filling Stir ingredients in small saucepan over heat, without boiling, until sugar dissolves. Simmer, uncovered, without stirring, about 10 minutes or until mixture is thick and syrupy; cool.

prep + cook time 40 minutes **serves** 6
tip Soufflés must be made just before serving.

caramel soufflés with walnut praline

3 eggs, separated
½ cup (110g) firmly packed brown sugar
1 tablespoon gelatine
¼ cup (60ml) water
⅓ cup (115g) golden syrup
300ml thickened cream, whipped
walnut praline
¼ cup (55g) caster sugar
¼ cup (25g) walnut pieces

1 Place a collar of foil around four ½ cup (125ml) soufflé dishes; secure with string. Brush inside of foil lightly with oil.
2 Beat egg yolks and sugar in heatproof bowl over simmering water until thick and creamy.
3 Sprinkle gelatine over the water in small jug; stand jug in small saucepan of simmering water, stir until dissolved. Stir gelatine mixture into egg mixture with golden syrup, stir over simmering water until combined. Remove from heat; transfer to large bowl. Cover; cool.
4 Fold cream into caramel mixture. Beat egg whites in small bowl with electric mixer until soft peaks form; fold into caramel mixture. Pour mixture into dishes; refrigerate until set.
5 Meanwhile, make walnut praline.
6 Remove foil collars from dishes, roll sides of soufflés in praline. Serve soufflés with remaining praline, if you like.
walnut praline Melt sugar in small heavy-based frying pan over heat; do not stir. When sugar starts to brown, stir gently to dissolve. Place nuts on greased oven tray, pour hot toffee evenly over nuts. When set, break into pieces; blend or process until finely ground.

prep + cook time 30 minutes (+ refrigeration) **serves** 4
tips These soufflés can be made a day ahead; keep, covered, in refrigerator. Decorate sides of soufflés with praline just before serving.

creamy marsala soufflés

3 egg yolks
⅓ cup (75g) caster sugar
¾ cup (180ml) milk
2 tablespoons marsala
3 teaspoons gelatine
¼ cup (60ml) water
300ml thickened cream

1 Place collar of foil around four ⅓ cup (80ml) dishes; secure with string. Brush inside of foil lightly with oil.
2 Beat egg yolks and sugar in small bowl with electric mixer until thick and creamy. Heat milk in small saucepan until almost boiling; gradually beat into egg yolk mixture.
3 Return mixture to pan, stir over heat, without boiling, until mixture begins to thicken. Transfer to large bowl; stir in marsala. Cover; cool to room temperature.
4 Sprinkle gelatine over water in small jug; stand jug in small saucepan of simmering water, stir until dissolved. Cool to room temperature; do not allow to set. Stir gelatine mixture into marsala mixture.
5 Beat cream in small bowl with electric mixer until soft peaks form; fold into marsala mixture in two batches.
6 Pour mixture into dishes; refrigerate for several hours or overnight. Remove collars from dishes, serve dusted with sifted cocoa.

prep + cook time 30 minutes (+ refrigeration) **serves** 4
tip These soufflés can be made a day ahead; keep, covered, in refrigerator.

rosewater soufflés

⅓ cup (75g) caster sugar
2 tablespoons water
2 tablespoons rosewater
300ml thickened cream
4 egg whites
2 teaspoons gelatine
1 tablespoon water, extra
pink food colouring, optional

1 Place collar of foil around four ½ cup (125ml) dishes; secure with string. Brush inside of foil lightly with oil.
2 Stir sugar and the water in small saucepan over heat, without boiling, until sugar dissolves. Remove from heat; stir in rosewater; cool. Refrigerate 30 minutes.
3 Beat cream and sugar syrup in medium bowl until soft peaks form. Beat egg whites in small bowl with electric mixer until firm peaks form; fold into cream mixture.
4 Sprinkle gelatine over water in small jug; stand jug in small saucepan of simmering water, stir until dissolved. Fold gelatine mixture into cream mixture, tint with colouring.
5 Spoon mixture into dishes; refrigerate until set. Remove collars from dishes, serve with whipped cream and rose petals, if you like.

prep + cook time 30 minutes (+ refrigeration) **serves** 4
tip These soufflés can be made a day ahead; keep, covered, in refrigerator.

mango soufflés with chocolate collars

100g dark eating chocolate, melted
50g butter, melted
3 eggs, separated
⅓ cup (75g) caster sugar
½ cup (125ml) milk
1½ cups (420g) fresh mango puree
1 tablespoon gelatine
¼ cup (60ml) water
300ml thickened cream

1 Place collar of foil around six ½ cup (125ml) dishes, about 1.5cm above the rim; secure with string. Brush inside of foil and halfway into dishes evenly with combined chocolate and butter; refrigerate until set.
2 Beat egg yolks and sugar in small bowl with electric mixer until thick and creamy. Heat milk in small saucepan until almost boiling; gradually beat into egg yolk mixture.
3 Return mixture to pan, stir over heat, without boiling, until mixture begins to thicken. Transfer to large bowl; cover, cool to room temperature.
4 Fold mango puree into custard. Sprinkle gelatine over water in small jug; stand jug in small saucepan of simmering water, stir until dissolved. Cool to room temperature; do not allow to set. Stir gelatine mixture into mango mixture.
5 Beat cream in small bowl of electric mixer until soft peaks form; fold into mango mixture.
6 Beat egg whites in small bowl of electric mixer until soft peaks form; fold into mango mixture.
7 Pour mixture into dishes; refrigerate until set. Remove collars, serve with whipped cream.

prep + cook time 40 minutes (+ refrigeration) **serves** 6
tips You will need about 3 medium mangoes (1.3kg) for this recipe. These soufflés can be made a day ahead; keep, covered, in refrigerator.

apricot and honey soufflés

¼ cup (55g) caster sugar
4 fresh medium apricots (200g)
¼ cup (60ml) water
2 tablespoons honey
4 egg whites
1 tablespoon icing sugar

1 Preheat oven to 180°C/160°C fan-forced. Grease six ¾ cup (180ml) soufflé dishes. Sprinkle inside of dishes with a little of the caster sugar; shake away excess. Place dishes on oven tray.
2 Place apricots in small heatproof bowl, cover with boiling water; stand 2 minutes. Drain; cool 5 minutes. Peel and seed apricots; chop flesh finely.
3 Combine apricot in small saucepan with remaining caster sugar, the water and honey; bring to a boil. Reduce heat, simmer, uncovered, about 10 minutes or until apricots soften to a jam-like consistency.
4 Beat egg whites in small bowl with electric mixer until soft peaks form. With motor operating, gradually add hot apricot mixture, beating until just combined.
5 Divide soufflé mixture among dishes; bake about 15 minutes. Serve immediately, dusted with sifted icing sugar.

prep + cook time 35 minutes **serves** 6
tip Soufflés must be made just before serving.

fresh apple soufflés

1½ tablespoons caster sugar
1 medium apple (150g), grated coarsely
2 tablespoons water
1 teaspoon finely grated lemon rind
1 tablespoon apricot jam
2 tablespoons caster sugar, extra
45g butter
1 tablespoon plain flour
1 tablespoon cornflour
¾ cup (180ml) milk
¼ cup (60ml) apple juice
3 eggs, separated

1 Preheat oven to 220°C/200°C fan-forced. Grease six ½ cup (125ml) soufflé dishes. Sprinkle inside of dishes with sugar; shake away excess. Place dishes on oven tray.
2 Stir apple, the water, rind, jam and extra sugar in small saucepan over heat, without boiling, until sugar dissolves; bring to the boil. Reduce heat; simmer, uncovered, without stirring, about 5 minutes or until apple is tender and liquid evaporates. Cool. Spoon apple mixture into dishes.
3 Melt butter in medium saucepan, add flours; stir over medium heat 1 minute. Remove from heat; gradually stir in milk and juice, stirring over high heat until mixture boils and thickens. Transfer mixture to large bowl; stir in egg yolks.
4 Beat egg whites in small bowl with electric mixer until soft peaks form; fold into egg yolk mixture, in two batches. Spoon mixture into dishes.
5 Bake soufflés about 20 minutes or until puffed and lightly browned. Serve immediately.

prep + cook time 40 minutes **serves** 6
tip Soufflés must be made just before serving.

coffee soufflés with pecan praline cream

1 tablespoon caster sugar
30g butter
1 tablespoon plain flour
¾ cup (180ml) hot milk
2 teaspoons instant coffee granules
2 egg yolks
¼ cup (55g) caster sugar, extra
3 egg whites
pecan praline cream
¼ cup (30g) pecans
¼ cup (60ml) water
2 tablespoons caster sugar
⅔ cup (160ml) thickened cream, whipped

1 Make pecan praline cream.
2 Preheat oven to 200°C/180°C fan-forced. Grease six ¾ cup (180ml)
soufflé dishes. Sprinkle inside of dishes with sugar; shake away excess.
Place dishes on oven tray.
3 Melt butter in medium saucepan, add flour; cook, stirring, over heat
until mixture bubbles and thickens. Remove from heat, gradually stir in
combined milk and coffee, stir over heat until mixture boils and thickens.
4 Meanwhile, beat egg yolks and sugar in small bowl with electric mixer
until thick and creamy; gradually beat in coffee mixture. Transfer mixture
to large bowl.
5 Beat egg whites in small bowl with electric mixer until soft peaks form;
fold into coffee mixture, in two batches. Pour mixture into dishes.
6 Bake soufflés about 15 minutes or until puffed and browned.
7 Serve soufflés immediately with praline cream.
pecan praline cream Place nuts on greased oven tray. Stir water and
sugar in small saucepan over heat, without boiling, until sugar dissolves.
Bring to the boil; boil, uncovered, without stirring, about 3 minutes or
until mixture turns golden brown. Quickly pour evenly over nuts; cool.
When set, break into pieces; blend or process until finely ground.
Combine praline and cream in small bowl.

prep + cook time 45 minutes **serves** 6
tip Soufflés must be made just before serving.

pear, red wine and honey soufflés

1 large pear (330g), peeled, cored, quartered
½ cup (125ml) water
½ cup (125ml) red wine
¼ cup (55g) caster sugar
¼ cup (90g) honey
4 egg whites

1 Preheat oven to 200°C/180°C fan-forced. Grease four 1 cup (250ml) ovenproof dishes; place on oven tray.
2 Place pear, the water and wine in small saucepan; bring to the boil. Reduce heat; simmer, uncovered, 20 minutes or until pear is tender and liquid has almost evaporated. Stir in sugar and honey. Cool slightly.
3 Blend pear mixture until smooth. Return mixture to pan, bring to the boil; boil, uncovered, without stirring, about 3 minutes or until mixture is thick and syrupy (you should end up with ⅔ cup of pulpy mixture).
4 Beat egg whites in small bowl with electric mixer until soft peaks form. Gradually pour hot pear mixture into egg whites while motor is operating. Spoon mixture into dishes.
5 Bake soufflés about 15 minutes or until puffed and golden brown. Serve immediately, dusted with sifted icing sugar.

prep + cook time 30 minutes **serves** 4
tip Soufflés must be made just before serving.

ginger soufflés

3 eggs, separated
¼ cup (55g) caster sugar
2 tablespoons plain flour
2 teaspoons ground ginger
¾ cup (180ml) boiling milk

1 Preheat oven to 200°C/180°C fan-forced. Grease six ½ cup (125ml) ovenproof dishes; place on oven tray.
2 Beat egg yolks and sugar in small heatproof bowl with electric mixer until thick and creamy; beat in sifted flour and ginger. Place bowl over small saucepan of simmering water; gradually whisk in milk, whisking over simmering water until thickened slightly. Transfer mixture to large bowl; cool 15 minutes.
3 Beat egg whites in small bowl with electric mixer until soft peaks form; fold into milk mixture in two batches. Pour mixture into dishes.
4 Bake soufflés about 15 minutes or until puffed and golden brown. Serve immediately, dusted with sifted icing sugar.

prep + cook time 30 minutes (+ cooling) **serves** 6
tip Soufflés must be made just before serving.

orange liqueur soufflés with macerated fruits

3 glacé apricots, chopped finely
3 rings glacé pineapple, chopped finely
2 tablespoons orange-flavoured liqueur
60g butter
2 tablespoons plain flour
2 teaspoons finely grated orange rind
¼ cup (55g) caster sugar
2 tablespoons orange-flavoured liqueur, extra
½ cup (125ml) milk
¼ cup (60ml) thickened cream
5 eggs, separated

1 Preheat oven to 200°C/180°C fan-forced. Grease six 1 cup (250ml) ovenproof dishes. Sprinkle inside of dishes with a little extra caster sugar; shake away excess. Place dishes on oven tray
2 Combine glacé fruit and liqueur in small bowl; cover, stand 30 minutes. Place fruit mixture into dishes.
3 Melt butter in medium saucepan, stir in flour; cook, stirring, over medium heat 1 minute. Remove from heat; gradually stir in combined rind, sugar, extra liqueur, milk and cream. Stir mixture over high heat until it boils and thickens. Remove from heat; transfer to large bowl, stir in egg yolks.
4 Beat egg whites in medium bowl with electric mixer until soft peaks form; fold into egg mixture, in two batches. Pour mixture into dishes.
5 Bake soufflés about 20 minutes or until puffed and golden brown. Serve immediately, dusted with sifted icing sugar.

prep + cook time 40 minutes (+ standing) **serves** 6
tip Soufflés must be made just before serving.

tangy lemon soufflé

90g butter, softened
1 tablespoon finely grated lemon rind
⅓ cup (75g) caster sugar
1 tablespoon plain flour
1 tablespoon cornflour
2 tablespoons lemon juice
1 cup (250ml) warm milk
4 eggs, separated
2 egg whites
1 tablespoon icing sugar

1 Preheat oven to 180°C/160°C fan-forced. Grease 1 litre (4 cup) soufflé dish; place on oven tray.
2 Beat butter, rind and caster sugar in small bowl with electric mixer until light and fluffy. Beat in sifted flours and juice; stir in milk. Transfer mixture to medium saucepan, stir over heat until mixture boils and thickens. Transfer mixture to large bowl; stir in egg yolks.
3 Beat all egg whites in medium bowl with electric mixer until soft peaks form; fold into lemon mixture in two batches. Pour mixture into dish.
4 Bake soufflé about 35 minutes or until puffed and browned. Serve immediately dusted with sifted icing sugar.

prep + cook time 50 minutes **serves** 6
tip Soufflés must be made just before serving.

hot raspberry soufflés

300g frozen raspberries, thawed
1 tablespoon water
½ cup (110g) caster sugar
4 egg whites
300ml thickened cream
2 teaspoons caster sugar, extra

1 Preheat oven to 180°C/160°C fan-forced. Grease four 1 cup (250ml) ovenproof dishes; place on oven tray.
2 Place 250g of the raspberries and the water in small saucepan; bring to the boil. Reduce heat; simmer, uncovered, until raspberries soften. Add sugar, stir over medium heat, without boiling, until sugar dissolves; bring to the boil. Reduce heat; simmer, uncovered, about 5 minutes or until mixture is thick and pulpy. Remove from heat; push mixture through fine sieve over small bowl, discard seeds.
3 Beat egg whites in small bowl with electric mixer until soft peaks form. With motor operating, gradually add hot raspberry mixture; beat until well combined. Divide mixture among dishes.
4 Bake soufflés about 15 minutes or until puffed and browned lightly.
5 Meanwhile, beat remaining raspberries, cream and extra sugar in small bowl with electric mixer until thickened slightly. Serve hot soufflés with raspberry cream.

prep + cook time 30 minutes **serves** 4
tips Soufflés must be made just before serving. Thaw raspberries on absorbent paper in the refrigerator.

blackberry soufflés

300g frozen blackberries
1 tablespoon water
⅓ cup (75g) caster sugar
4 egg whites
1 tablespoon icing sugar

1 Preheat oven to 200°C/180°C fan-forced. Grease four 1 cup (250ml) ovenproof dishes; place on oven tray.
2 Place blackberries and the water in small saucepan; bring to the boil. Reduce heat; simmer, uncovered, until blackberries soften. Add caster sugar, stir over medium heat, without boiling, until sugar dissolves; bring to the boil. Reduce heat; simmer, uncovered, 5 minutes. Remove from heat; using the back of a large spoon, push blackberry mixture through sieve into small bowl, discarding seeds in sieve. Refrigerate 15 minutes.
3 Beat egg whites in medium bowl with electric mixer until soft peaks form. Fold in berry mixture until combined. Divide mixture among dishes.
4 Bake soufflés about 12 minutes or until puffed and browned lightly. Serve immediately, dusted with sifted icing sugar.

prep + cook time 30 minutes (+ refrigeration) **serves** 4
tip Soufflés must be made just before serving.

hot passionfruit soufflé with raspberry cream

1 tablespoon caster sugar
2 eggs, separated
½ cup passionfruit pulp
2 tablespoons lemon juice
¾ cup (120g) icing sugar
4 egg whites
raspberry cream
125g frozen raspberries, thawed
300ml thickened cream
1 tablespoon icing sugar
1 tablespoon orange-flavoured liqueur

1 Make raspberry cream; refrigerate until required.
2 Preheat oven to 220°C/200°C fan-forced. Grease four 1 cup (250ml) soufflé dishes, sprinkle inside each one with caster sugar; shake away excess. Place dishes on oven tray.
3 Combine yolks, passionfruit, juice and half of the sifted icing sugar in large bowl.
4 Beat all the egg whites in small bowl with electric mixer until soft peaks form; add remaining sifted icing sugar and continue beating until firm peaks form. Gently fold a quarter of the whites into passionfruit mixture, then fold in remaining whites. Spoon mixture into dishes.
5 Bake soufflés about 10 minutes or until puffed and browned.
6 Dust soufflés with a little extra sifted icing sugar, if you like. Serve immediately with raspberry cream.
raspberry cream Push thawed raspberries through sieve to remove seeds. Whip cream and icing sugar until soft peaks form; fold in raspberry puree and liqueur.

prep + cook time 30 minutes **serves** 4
tips You will need about six passionfruit for this recipe. Soufflés must be made just before serving.

pink grapefruit soufflés

⅓ cup (75g) caster sugar
⅓ cup (50g) plain flour
¾ cup (180ml) skim milk
1 tablespoon finely grated pink grapefruit rind
¼ cup (60ml) pink grapefruit juice
1 teaspoon grenadine
20g butter
3 egg yolks
5 egg whites
1 tablespoon icing sugar

1 Preheat oven to 220°C/200°C fan-forced. Grease six ¾ cup (180ml) ovenproof dishes, sprinkle bases and sides of dishes with a little of the caster sugar; shake away excess. Place on oven tray.
2 Place remaining caster sugar with flour in medium saucepan, gradually whisk in milk; cook, stirring, until mixture boils and thickens. Whisk in rind, juice, grenadine and butter; remove from heat. Transfer mixture to large bowl; whisk in egg yolks, one at a time.
3 Beat egg whites in medium bowl with electric mixer until soft peaks form; fold into grapefruit mixture, in two batches. Divide mixture among dishes.
4 Bake soufflés about 15 minutes or until puffed and brown. Serve immediately, dusted with icing sugar.

prep + cook time 30 minutes **serves** 6
tips Grenadine is a deep-red syrup based on pomegranate juice and used to both colour and sweeten desserts and drinks. Some types of grenadine contain alcohol; the one we used did not. You could also use raspberry cordial or topping instead of the grenadine to enhance the pink colour.

DESSERT CAKES

fig and almond cake with butterscotch sauce

1½ cups (285g) finely chopped
   dried figs
1½ cups (375ml) water
1 teaspoon bicarbonate soda
125g unsalted butter, softened
1 cup (220g) caster sugar
3 eggs
1 cup (150g) self-raising flour
½ cup (60g) ground almonds
¼ cup (40g) finely chopped
   blanched almonds

butterscotch sauce
1 cup (220g) firmly packed
   brown sugar
1 cup (250ml) cream
150g unsalted butter
1 tablespoon irish cream liqueur

1 Preheat oven to 180°C/160°C fan-forced. Grease deep 22cm round cake pan; line base with baking paper.
2 Bring figs and the water to the boil in small saucepan. Remove from heat, add soda; cover, stand 5 minutes. Blend or process until smooth.
3 Beat butter and sugar in small bowl with electric mixer until light and fluffy; beat in eggs one at a time. Transfer mixture to large bowl; stir in sifted flour, ground almonds and chopped nuts, then fig mixture. Pour mixture into pan.
4 Bake cake about 1 hour. Stand cake in pan 10 minutes before turning onto wire rack to cool.
5 Meanwhile, make butterscotch cream
6 Serve cake, sliced with butterscotch sauce and whipped cream.
butterscotch sauce Stir ingredients in small saucepan over heat, without boiling, until sugar dissolves. Simmer, without stirring, 3 minutes.

prep + cook time 1 hour 30 minutes **serves** 12

cumquat and almond dessert cake

600g cumquats
2 cups (320g) blanched almonds, roasted
6 eggs
1 cup (220g) caster sugar
¼ cup (40g) semolina
1 teaspoon baking powder
crème anglaise
1¾ cups (430ml) milk
4 egg yolks
¼ cup (55g) caster sugar
1 teaspoon vanilla extract

1 Preheat oven to 180°C/160°C fan-forced. Grease 24cm springform tin; line base with baking paper. Sprinkle sides of tin with a little flour; shake away excess flour, stand tin on oven tray.
2 Simmer whole cumquats, covered, in medium saucepan of boiling water, 1 hour or until very soft. Drain.
3 Halve cumquats; discard seeds. Blend or process cumquats until smooth. Process almonds until finely chopped.
4 Beat eggs and sugar in medium bowl with electric mixer until pale and thick. Fold in cumquat puree, ground almonds, semolina and sifted baking powder. Pour mixture into tin.
5 Bake cake about 1 hour. Stand cake in pan 10 minutes before turning onto wire rack to cool.
6 Meanwhile, make crème anglaise.
7 Serve cake dusted with sifted icing sugar and crème anglaise.
crème anglaise Bring milk to the boil in medium saucepan. Whisk egg yolks and sugar in medium bowl until creamy; gradually whisk into hot milk. Stir over heat, without boiling, until mixture thickens slightly; stir in extract.

prep + cook time 2 hours 30 minutes **serves** 8

citrus almond syrup cake

2 medium oranges (360g)
1½ cups (240g) almond kernels
1 cup (220g) caster sugar
6 eggs
1 teaspoon baking powder
1 teaspoon vanilla extract
lime syrup
½ cup (110g) caster sugar
¼ cup (60ml) lime juice
¼ cup (60ml) water

1 Place whole oranges in medium saucepan, add enough hot water to cover oranges. Cover, bring to boil, then simmer about 2 hours, or until oranges are tender. Replenish water with boiling water as it evaporates during cooking. Drain oranges, cool; discard water.

2 Preheat oven to 160°C/140°C fan-forced. Grease deep 20cm round cake pan; line base with baking paper.

3 Process almonds and sugar until almonds are roughly chopped; transfer mixture to medium bowl.

4 Quarter whole oranges, blend or process until smooth. With motor operating, add eggs one at a time, process until combined. Add almond mixture, baking powder and extract, process until just combined. Spread mixture into pan.

5 Bake cake about 1 hour.

6 Make lime syrup; pour hot syrup over hot cake. Stand cake in pan 30 minutes. Turn cake onto wire rack over tray. Serve warm or cold.

lime syrup Stir ingredients in small saucepan over heat, without boiling, until sugar dissolves. Simmer, uncovered, without stirring, about 5 minutes or until slightly thickened.

prep + cook time 3 hours 20 minutes (+ standing) **serves** 8

warm apple cake with brandy butterscotch sauce

125g butter, chopped
½ cup (110g) caster sugar
2 eggs
⅔ cup (100g) self-raising flour
⅓ cup (50g) plain flour
1 tablespoon milk
3 medium granny smith apples (450g)
½ cup (160g) apricot jam, warmed
brandy butterscotch sauce
½ cup (100g) firmly packed brown sugar
½ cup (125ml) thickened cream
100g butter, chopped
2 tablespoons brandy

1 Preheat oven to 160°C/140°C fan-forced. Grease two 8cm x 26cm bar cake pans; line base and sides with baking paper.
2 Beat butter and sugar in small bowl with electric mixer until light and fluffy. Beat in eggs, one at a time, beating until combined between each addition. Stir in sifted flours and milk; spread mixture into pans.
3 Peel, core and halve apples; slice halves thinly. Push apple slices gently into surface of cake mixture. Brush apple with strained jam.
4 Bake cakes about 40 minutes. Stand cakes 10 minutes before turning, top-side up, onto wire rack to cool.
5 Meanwhile, make brandy butterscotch sauce.
6 Serve pieces of cake warm, drizzled with sauce.
brandy butterscotch sauce Stir ingredients in small saucepan over heat, without boiling, until sugar dissolves; bring to the boil. Reduce heat; simmer, uncovered, without stirring, about 3 minute or until mixture thickens slightly.

prep + cook time 1 hour **serves** 8
tip Peel, core and cut apples just before using to prevent the flesh from going brown.

dark chocolate and almond torte

160g dark eating chocolate, chopped coarsely
160g unsalted butter
5 eggs, separated
¾ cup (165g) caster sugar
1 cup (125g) ground almond
⅔ cup (50g) roasted flaked almonds, chopped coarsely
⅓ cup (35g) coarsely grated dark eating chocolate
1 cup (140g) vienna almonds
dark chocolate ganache
125g dark eating chocolate, chopped coarsely
⅓ cup (80ml) thickened cream

1 Preheat oven to 180°C/160°C fan-forced. Grease deep 22cm-round cake pan; line base and side with two layers of baking paper.
2 Stir chopped chocolate and butter in small saucepan over low heat until smooth; cool to room temperature.
3 Beat egg yolks and sugar in small bowl with electric mixer until thick and creamy. Transfer to large bowl; fold in chocolate mixture, ground almonds, flaked almonds and grated chocolate.
4 Beat egg whites in small bowl with electric mixer until soft peaks form; fold into chocolate mixture, in two batches. Pour mixture into pan.
5 Bake cake about 45 minutes. Stand cake in pan 15 minutes before turning onto wire rack; turn top-side up to cool.
6 Meanwhile, make dark chocolate ganache.
7 Spread ganache over cake, decorate cake with vienna almonds; stand 30 minutes before serving.
dark chocolate ganache Stir ingredients in small saucepan over low heat until smooth.

prep + cook time 1 hour (+ cooling and standing) **serves** 14
tip This cake can be stored in refrigerator for up to 2 days. Uniced, this cake is suitable to freeze for up to 3 months.

moist whole orange cake

2 medium oranges (480g)
⅔ cup (110g) blanched almonds, roasted
1 cup (220g) caster sugar
1 teaspoon baking powder
6 eggs
2 cups (250g) ground almonds
2 tablespoons plain flour

1 Place unpeeled oranges in medium saucepan; cover with cold water, bring to the boil. Boil, covered, 30 minutes; drain. Repeat process with fresh water, boil about 1 hour or until oranges are tender; cool.
2 Preheat oven to 180°C/160°C fan-forced. Grease deep 22cm-round cake pan; line base and side with baking paper.
3 Process roasted blanched almonds with 2 tablespoons of the sugar until finely chopped.
4 Trim ends off oranges and discard. Halve oranges; remove and discard seeds. Process oranges, including rind, with baking powder until mixture is pulpy.
5 Beat eggs and remaining sugar in medium bowl with electric mixer about 3 minutes or until fluffy and pale in colour. Fold in almond mixture, ground almonds, flour and orange pulp. Pour mixture into pan.
6 Bake cake about 1 hour or until cooked when tested. Cool in pan. Serve dusted with icing sugar.

prep + cook time 3 hours **serves** 10
tip This cake can be stored in an airtight container for up to 2 days. This cake is suitable to freeze for up to 3 months.

hummingbird cake

450g can crushed pineapple in syrup
1 cup (150g) plain flour
½ cup (75g) self-raising flour
½ teaspoon bicarbonate of soda
½ teaspoon ground cinnamon
½ teaspoon ground ginger
1 cup (220g) firmly packed brown sugar
½ cup (45g) desiccated coconut
1 cup mashed banana
2 eggs
¾ cup (180ml) vegetable oil
cream cheese frosting
30g butter, softened
60g cream cheese, softened
1 teaspoon vanilla extract
1½ cups (240g) icing sugar

1 Preheat oven to 180°C/160°C fan-forced. Grease deep 23cm-square cake pan; line base with baking paper.
2 Drain pineapple over medium bowl, pressing with spoon to extract as much syrup as possible. Reserve ¼ cup (60ml) syrup.
3 Sift flours, soda, spices and sugar into large bowl. Stir in drained pineapple, reserved syrup, coconut, banana, eggs and oil. Pour mixture into pan.
4 Bake cake about 40 minutes. Stand cake in pan 5 minutes; turn, top-side up, onto wire rack to cool.
5 Meanwhile, make cream cheese frosting; spread cake with frosting.
cream cheese frosting Beat butter, cream cheese and extract in small bowl with electric mixer until light and fluffy; gradually beat in sifted icing sugar.

prep + cook time 1 hour **serves** 12
tips You need about 2 large overripe (460g) bananas for this recipe. The pineapple must be well drained; too much syrup will give you a heavy cake. Cake will keep for up to 3 days in an airtight container in the refrigerator. Frosted or unfrosted, the cake can be frozen for up to 3 months.

passionfruit sponge roll

3 eggs
½ cup (110g) caster sugar
1 teaspoon vanilla extract
¾ cup (100g) wheaten cornflour
¾ teaspoon cream of tartar
½ teaspoon bicarbonate of soda
¼ cup (10g) flaked coconut
¼ cup (55g) caster sugar, extra
½ cup (125ml) thickened cream
1 teaspoon icing sugar

passionfruit curd
⅓ cup (80ml) passionfruit pulp
⅔ cup (150g) caster sugar
2 eggs, beaten lightly
125g unsalted butter, chopped

1 Preheat oven to 180°C/160°C fan-forced. Grease 25cm x 30cm swiss roll pan; line base with baking paper, extending paper 5cm over long sides.

2 Beat eggs, caster sugar and extract in small bowl with electric mixer until sugar is dissolved. Fold in triple-sifted cornflour, cream of tartar and soda. Spread mixture into pan; sprinkle with coconut. Bake about 12 minutes.

3 Meanwhile, place a piece of baking paper cut the same size as pan on bench; sprinkle evenly with extra caster sugar. Turn sponge onto paper; peel lining paper away. Cool; trim all sides of sponge.

4 Meanwhile, make passionfruit curd.

5 Whip cream and icing sugar in small bowl with electric mixer until soft peaks form. Unroll sponge; spread with half the passionfruit curd, top with cream. Using paper as a guide, roll sponge from long side.

passionfruit curd Stir ingredients in medium heatproof bowl over medium saucepan of simmering water about 10 minutes or until thickened slightly. Remove from heat; cool.

prep + cook time 30 minutes (+ cooling) **serves** 6
tips Sponge is best made on day of serving and is not suitable to freeze. Passionfruit curd can be made 3 days ahead.

coffee caramel cakes

125g butter, softened
⅔ cup (150g) firmly packed brown sugar
2 tablespoons instant coffee granules
1 tablespoon boiling water
2 eggs
2 cups (300g) self-raising flour
½ cup (125ml) milk
18 (130g) jersey caramels, halved

1 Preheat oven to 180°C/160°C fan-forced. Grease 12-hole (⅓-cup/80ml) muffin pan.
2 Beat butter and sugar in small bowl with electric mixer until light and fluffy. Add combined coffee and the water; beat in eggs, one at a time. Transfer mixture to large bowl; stir in sifted flour and milk.
3 Spoon mixture into pan holes. Press 3 caramel halves into the centre of each cake; cover with batter.
4 Bake cakes about 20 minutes. Stand cakes in pan 5 minutes; turn, top-side up, onto wire racks to cool.

prep + cook time 40 minutes (+ cooling) **makes** 12
tips These cakes are best made on day of serving. They can be frozen for up to 1 month.

cardamom orange mousse cakes

50g dark eating chocolate, melted
25g unsalted butter, melted
125g butternut snap biscuits
25g unsalted butter, melted, extra
1 teaspoon finely grated
  orange rind
¼ teaspoon ground cardamom

orange mousse
300ml thickened cream
150g dark eating chocolate,
  chopped coarsely
1 teaspoon finely grated
  orange rind
¼ teaspoon ground cardamom
orange syrup
⅔ cup (160ml) orange juice
¼ cup (55g) caster sugar
2 tablespoons finely shredded
  orange rind

1 Make orange mousse.
2 Grease 12-hole (¼ cup/60ml) mini cheesecake pan with removable bases; line bases with baking paper.
3 Combine chocolate and butter, spoon into holes; cool 5 minutes.
4 Process biscuits until fine. Add extra butter, rind and cardamom; process until combined. Divide mixture among pan holes; press firmly over chocolate bases.
5 Divide mousse among pan holes; refrigerate overnight.
6 Make orange syrup.
7 Serve mousse cakes with orange syrup.
orange mousse Stir ingredients in small heatproof bowl over small saucepan of simmering water until smooth. Refrigerate 30 minutes or until cool. Beat mousse mixture with electric mixer for 2 minutes or until mixture changes to a paler colour. Do not overbeat or mixture will curdle.
orange syrup Stir juice and sugar in small saucepan, over heat, without boiling, until sugar dissolves. Add rind; bring to the boil. Reduce heat; simmer, uncovered, about 10 minutes or until syrup thickens slightly. Cool.

prep + cook time 45 minutes (+ cooling and refrigeration) **makes** 12

chocolate fondants

200g dark eating chocolate, chopped coarsely
100g unsalted butter, chopped coarsely
1 tablespoon cocoa powder
1 tablespoon self-raising flour
⅓ cup (75g) caster sugar
3 eggs

1 Grease 6-hole (½ cup/125ml) friand pan evenly with a little melted butter.
2 Stir chocolate and butter in small heatproof bowl over small saucepan of simmering water until smooth.
3 Sift cocoa, flour and sugar into medium bowl; whisk in eggs and chocolate mixture.
4 Divide mixture between pan holes; cover pan with foil, freeze 3 hours or overnight.
5 Preheat oven to 220°C/200°C fan-forced.
6 Bake frozen fondants 7 minutes; turn pan, bake further 7 minutes. Stand fondants 2 minutes; loosen edges with knife, gently ease out of pan. Serve immediately with cream or ice-cream.

prep + cook time 30 minutes (+ freezing) **makes** 6
tips These are the perfect do-ahead desserts; they can be frozen, ready-to-bake, weeks ahead. Make sure you're organised so the fondants are served and eaten while their centre is wonderfully soft and gooey.

upside down toffee date and banana cake

1½ cups (330g) caster sugar
1½ cups (375ml) water
3 star anise
2 medium bananas (400g),
   sliced thinly
1 cup (140g) dried seeded dates
¾ cup (180ml) water, extra
½ cup (125ml) dark rum
1 teaspoon bicarbonate of soda

60g butter, chopped
½ cup (110g) firmly packed
   brown sugar
2 eggs
2 teaspoons mixed spice
1 cup (150g) self-raising flour
½ cup mashed banana
300ml thickened cream

1 Preheat oven to 180°C/160°C fan-forced. Grease deep 22cm-round cake pan; line base with baking paper.

2 Stir caster sugar, the water and star anise in medium saucepan over low heat, without boiling, until sugar dissolves. Bring to the boil; boil syrup, uncovered, without stirring, about 5 minutes or until thickened slightly. Strain ½ cup of the syrup into small heatproof jug; reserve to flavour cream. Discard star anise.

3 To make toffee, continue boiling remaining syrup, uncovered, without stirring, about 10 minutes or until golden brown. Pour hot toffee into cake pan; top with sliced banana.

4 Place dates, the extra water and rum in small saucepan; bring to the boil, remove from heat. Stir in soda; stand 5 minutes. Process date mixture with butter and brown sugar until almost smooth. Add eggs, spice and flour; process until just combined. Stir in mashed banana. Pour mixture into pan.

5 Bake cake about 40 minutes. Turn cake, in pan, onto serving plate; stand 2 minutes. Remove pan then peel away baking paper.

6 To make star anise cream, beat cream in small bowl with electric mixer until firm peaks form. Stir in reserved syrup.

7 Serve cake warm or at room temperature with star anise cream.

prep + cook time 1 hour 30 minutes **serves** 12

tips Make sure that the bananas you choose to mash for the cake mixture are overripe; if they're not, they won't mash easily and can cause the cake to be too heavy. We prefer to use an underproof rum in baking because of its more subtle flavour; however, you can use an overproof rum and still get satisfactory results.

semolina and yogurt lemon-syrup cake

250g butter
1 tablespoon finely grated lemon rind
1 cup (220g) caster sugar
3 eggs, separated
1 cup (150g) self-raising flour
1 cup (160g) semolina
1 cup (280g) yogurt
lemon syrup
1 cup (220g) caster sugar
⅓ cup (80ml) lemon juice

1 Preheat oven to 180°C/160°C fan-forced. Grease and flour 20cm baba pan (or deep 19cm-round cake pan); shake away excess flour.
2 Beat butter, rind and sugar in small bowl with electric mixer until light and fluffy. Beat in egg yolks. Transfer mixture to large bowl; stir in flour, semolina and yogurt.
3 Beat egg whites in small bowl with electric mixer until soft peaks form; fold egg whites into cake mixture, in two batches. Spread mixture into pan; bake about 50 minutes.
4 Meanwhile, make lemon syrup.
5 Stand cake 5 minutes; turn onto wire rack set over tray. Pierce cake all over with skewer; pour hot syrup over hot cake.
lemon syrup Stir ingredients in small saucepan over heat until sugar dissolves. Bring to the boil without stirring; remove from heat.

prep + cook time 1 hour (+ cooling) **serves** 8

sticky date roll with butterscotch sauce

2 tablespoons white sugar
1 cup (160g) seeded dates
¾ cup (180ml) boiling water
1 teaspoon bicarbonate of soda
50g butter, chopped
⅔ cup (150g) firmly packed brown sugar
2 eggs
¾ cup (110g) self-raising flour
300ml thickened cream
butterscotch sauce
½ cup (100g) firmly packed brown sugar
⅔ cup (160ml) thickened cream
100g butter, chopped

1 Preheat oven to 180°C/160°C fan-forced. Grease 25cm x 30cm swiss roll pan; line base with baking paper, extending paper 5cm over short sides. Place a piece of baking paper cut the same size as pan on bench; sprinkle evenly with white sugar.
2 Place dates, the water and soda in bowl of food processor. Cover with lid; stand 5 minutes. Add butter and brown sugar; process until almost smooth. Add eggs and flour; process until just combined.
3 Pour mixture into pan; bake about 15 minutes. Turn sponge onto sugared paper; peel lining paper away. Trim all sides of sponge. Using hands and sugared paper as a guide, gently roll cake loosely from a long side; hold for 30 seconds then unroll. Cover cake with tea towel; cool.
4 Make butterscotch sauce.
5 Beat cream in small bowl with electric mixer until firm peaks form. Fold ¼ cup of the butterscotch sauce into cream. Spread cake evenly with cream mixture. Roll cake, from same long side, by lifting paper and using it to guide the roll into shape. Serve sticky date roll drizzled with remaining warmed sauce.
butterscotch sauce Stir ingredients in small saucepan over heat until sugar dissolves and butter melts.

prep + cook time 40 minutes (+ cooling) **serves** 12
tip Rolling and unrolling the cake, then cooling it flat, is not the traditional method for a swiss roll; however, it does help minimise the likelihood of the cake splitting.

maple pecan cake

cooking-oil spray
1 cup (100g) pecans
⅓ cup (80ml) maple syrup
1¼ cups (235g) coarsely chopped dried figs
1¼ cups (310ml) boiling water
1 teaspoon bicarbonate of soda
60g butter
¾ cup (150g) firmly packed brown sugar
2 eggs
1 cup (150g) self-raising flour
maple butterscotch sauce
1 cup (250ml) maple syrup
½ cup (125ml) cream
100g butter, chopped

1 Preheat oven to 180°C/160°C fan-forced. Grease deep 20cm-round cake pan; line base with baking paper. Spray paper with oil.
2 Arrange nuts over base of pan; drizzle with maple syrup.
3 Place figs, the water and soda in bowl of food processor. Cover with lid; stand 5 minutes. Add butter and sugar; process until almost smooth. Add eggs and flour; process until just combined. Pour mixture into pan.
4 Bake cake about 55 minutes. Stand cake 5 minutes; turn onto wire rack to cool.
5 Meanwhile, make maple butterscotch sauce.
6 Serve cake with sauce and vanilla ice-cream.

maple butterscotch sauce Stir ingredients in small saucepan over heat until smooth; bring to the boil. Boil, uncovered, about 2 minutes or until mixture thickens slightly.

prep + cook time 1 hour **serves** 10
tip You can use either pure maple syrup or maple-flavoured syrup in this recipe.

apricot upside down cakes

1 tablespoon brown sugar
12 canned apricot halves in syrup, drained
2 eggs
¾ cup (150g) firmly packed brown sugar, extra
¾ cup (90g) ground almonds
1 teaspoon vanilla extract
⅓ cup (50g) wholemeal self-raising flour
½ cup (125ml) no-fat milk
¼ cup (80g) light apricot conserve, warmed

1 Preheat oven to 180°C/160°C fan-forced. Grease 12-hole (⅓ cup/ 80ml) muffin pan.
2 Sprinkle sugar equally into pan holes; place one apricot half, cut-side down, into each hole.
3 Beat eggs and extra sugar in medium bowl with electric mixer until light and fluffy. Stir in ground almonds, extract, flour and milk. Divide mixture into pan holes.
4 Bake cakes about 20 minutes. Stand 5 minutes; turn onto wire rack. Brush apricot conserve over hot cakes. Serve cakes warm or at room temperature.

prep + cook time 40 minutes **makes** 12
tip You'll probably have to open a 415g can of apricot halves to get the required amount for this recipe. Serve the remaining apricot halves with the cakes.

chocolate mocha dacquoise terrine

4 egg whites
1 cup (220g) caster sugar
2 tablespoons cocoa powder
200g dark eating chocolate,
  chopped coarsely
¾ cup (180ml) cream
2 teaspoons cocoa powder, extra

mocha butter cream
1 tablespoon instant coffee
  granules
2 tablespoons boiling water
100g unsalted butter
2¼ cups (360g) icing sugar

1 Preheat oven to 150°C/130°C fan-forced. Line each of three oven trays with baking paper; draw a 10cm x 25cm rectangle on each piece of baking paper.
2 Beat egg whites in medium bowl with electric mixer until soft peaks form. Gradually add sugar, beating after each addition until sugar dissolves; fold in sifted cocoa. Spread meringue mixture evenly over drawn rectangles.
3 Bake meringues about 45 minutes or until they are dry. Turn off oven; cool meringues in oven with door ajar.
4 Meanwhile, stir chocolate and cream in small saucepan over low heat until smooth; transfer to small bowl. Refrigerate until firm. Beat chocolate mixture with electric mixer about 20 seconds or until just changed in colour.
5 Make mocha butter cream.
6 Place one meringue layer on serving plate; spread with half of the chocolate mixture, then top with half of the butter cream. Top with another meringue layer; spread with remaining chocolate mixture, then with remaining butter cream. Top with last meringue layer, cover; refrigerate 3 hours or overnight. Serve dusted with extra sifted cocoa powder.
mocha butter cream Dissolve coffee in the boiling water in small bowl; cool 10 minutes. Beat butter in small bowl with electric mixer until pale in colour; gradually add sugar, beating until combined. Beat in coffee mixture.

prep + cook time 1 hour (+ refrigeration) **serves** 12

pear crumble cake

2 cups (500ml) water
1 cup (220g) caster sugar
2 cinnamon sticks
2 small pears (360g), sliced thinly
125g butter
⅔ cup (150g) caster sugar, extra
2 eggs
1½ cups (225g) self-raising flour
crumble topping
½ cup (75g) plain flour
⅓ cup (75g) caster sugar
60g butter
½ cup (45g) desiccated coconut

1 Preheat oven to 180°C/160°C fan-forced. Grease 22cm springform tin; line base and side with foil.
2 Stir the water, sugar and cinnamon in medium saucepan over heat, without boiling, until sugar dissolves. Add pears; simmer about 5 minutes or until just tender. Drain on absorbent paper.
3 Meanwhile, make crumble topping.
4 Beat butter and extra sugar in small bowl with electric mixer until light and fluffy. Beat in eggs, one at a time. Add flour; beat until combined. Spread mixture into pan; top cake mixture with half the pears, sprinkle with half the crumble topping. Repeat with remaining pears and crumble.
5 Bake cake about 1 hour. Cool cake in pan.
crumble topping Blend or process all ingredients until fine and crumbly.

prep + cook time 1 hour 30 minutes (+ cooling) **serves** 10
tip It is important to slice pears as thinly as possible; if the slices are too thick, the cake will sink in the centre.

blueberry cake with vanilla syrup

125g butter
½ cup (110g) caster sugar
2 eggs
1¾ cups (260g) self-raising flour
½ cup (125ml) buttermilk
¾ cup (110g) frozen blueberries
vanilla syrup
½ cup (110g) caster sugar
½ cup (125ml) water
2 teaspoons vanilla extract

1 Preheat oven to 180°C/160°C fan-forced. Grease deep 20cm ring cake pan; line base and side with baking paper.
2 Beat butter and sugar in medium bowl with electric mixer until light and fluffy. Beat in eggs one at a time. Stir in flour and buttermilk, in two batches. Spread mixture into pan, sprinkle with frozen berries, gently pressing into cake mixture.
3 Bake cake about 45 minutes. Stand cake in pan 5 minutes, before turning onto wire rack over tray.
4 Make vanilla syrup; drizzle hot syrup over hot cake.
vanilla syrup Stir sugar and water in small saucepan over heat, without boiling, until sugar dissolves. Simmer, uncovered, without stirring, 2 minutes. Stir in extract; transfer to heatproof jug.

prep + cook time 1 hour (+ standing) **serves** 8
tip Use blueberries while they're still frozen.

chocolate pudding cake

370g chocolate cake mix
100g chocolate instant pudding dessert mix
¼ cup (60ml) vegetable oil
60g unsalted butter, softened
3 eggs
¾ cup (180ml) water

1 Preheat oven to 180°C/160°C fan-forced. Grease 21cm baba pan.
2 Place cake mix and pudding mix into small bowl with remaining ingredients (do not add ingredients listed on packets). Follow method for mixing on cake mix packet. Pour mixture into pan.
3 Bake cake about 50 minutes. Stand in pan 5 minutes before turning onto wire rack to cool.

prep + cook time 1 hour 10 minutes **serves** 8
tip Use a cake mix that does not require butter to be added.

orange and date dessert muffins

2 cups (300g) self-raising flour
½ cup (75g) plain flour
½ teaspoon bicarbonate of soda
1¼ cups (250g) firmly packed brown sugar
125g butter, melted
1 cup (250ml) buttermilk
1 egg, beaten lightly
2 teaspoons finely grated orange rind
1 cup (160g) coarsely chopped seeded dates
orange sauce
¾ cup (150g) firmly packed brown sugar
2 teaspoons cornflour
⅓ cup (80ml) orange juice
2 tablespoons orange-flavoured liqueur
125g butter, chopped
1 tablespoon finely grated orange rind

1 Preheat oven to 200°C/180°C fan-forced. Line 12-hole (⅓-cup/80ml) muffin pan with paper cases.
2 Sift flours and soda into large bowl, stir in sugar. Stir in butter, buttermilk, egg, rind and dates until just combined. Divide mixture between paper cases.
3 Bake muffins about 20 minutes. Stand in pan 5 minutes.
4 Meanwhile, make orange sauce.
5 Serve muffins warm with orange sauce.
orange sauce Combine sugar and cornflour in small saucepan, gradually stir in juice and liqueur; bring to the boil, stirring until sauce boils and thickens. Stir in butter and rind.

prep + cook time 30 minutes **makes** 12

361

raspberry hazelnut cake

250g butter, softened
2 cups (440g) caster sugar
6 eggs
1 cup (150g) plain flour
½ cup (75g) self-raising flour
1 cup (100g) ground hazelnuts
⅔ cup (160g) sour cream
300g fresh or frozen raspberries
mascarpone cream
1 cup (250g) mascarpone
¼ cup (40g) icing sugar
2 tablespoons hazelnut-flavoured liqueur
½ cup (120g) sour cream
½ cup (70g) roasted hazelnuts, chopped finely

1 Preheat oven to 180°C/160°C fan-forced. Grease deep 22cm-round cake pan; line base and side with baking paper.
2 Beat butter and sugar in medium bowl with electric mixer until light and fluffy. Beat in eggs, one at a time (mixture will curdle at this stage, but will come together later). Transfer mixture to large bowl; stir in sifted flours, ground hazelnuts, sour cream and raspberries. Spread mixture into pan.
3 Bake cake about 1½ hours. Stand cake in pan 10 minutes; turn, top-side up, onto wire rack to cool.
4 Meanwhile, make mascarpone cream.
5 Place cold cake on serving plate; spread mascarpone cream all over cake.
mascarpone cream Stir mascarpone, icing sugar, liqueur and sour cream in medium bowl until smooth; stir in nuts.

prep + cook time 2 hours (+ cooling) **serves** 12
tips If using frozen raspberries, don't thaw them; frozen berries are less likely to "bleed" into the cake mixture. Cake can be frosted the day before required; store, covered, in refrigerator. Unfrosted cake will keep for up to 3 days in an airtight container at room temperature. Unfrosted cake can be frozen for up to 3 months.

irish pudding cake

1½ cups (210g) seeded dried
  dates, chopped coarsely
1¼ cups (210g) seeded prunes,
  chopped coarsely
1½ cups (225g) raisins,
  chopped coarsely
1 cup (110g) dried currants
¾ cup (120g) sultanas
1 large apple (200g),
  grated coarsely
1½ cups (375ml) irish whiskey

1¼ cups (275g) firmly packed
  dark brown sugar
185g butter, softened
3 eggs, beaten lightly
½ cup (50g) ground hazelnuts
1½ cups (225g) plain flour
1 teaspoon ground nutmeg
½ teaspoon ground ginger
½ teaspoon ground cloves
½ teaspoon bicarbonate of soda

1 Combine fruit and 1 cup of the whiskey in large bowl. Cover tightly
with plastic wrap; stand at room temperature overnight.
2 Preheat oven to 120°C/100°C fan-forced. Grease deep 20cm-round
cake pan; line base and side of pan with two thicknesses of baking paper,
extending paper 5cm above side.
3 Stir remaining whiskey and ½ cup of the sugar in small saucepan
over heat until sugar dissolves; bring to the boil. Remove from heat;
cool 20 minutes.
4 Meanwhile, beat butter and remaining sugar in small bowl with electric
mixer until just combined (do not overbeat). Beat in eggs, one at a time.
Add butter mixture to fruit mixture; stir in ground hazelnuts, sifted dry
ingredients and ½ cup of the cooled syrup. Spread mixture into pan.
5 Bake cake about 3 hours. Brush cake with reheated remaining syrup;
cover hot cake with foil, cool in pan overnight.

prep + cook time 3 hours 30 minutes (+ cooling and standing)
serves 16
tips This cake will keep, covered, in the refrigerator for up to a month.
Although the inclusion of Irish whiskey makes it authentic, scotch, dark
rum or brandy are fine substitutes.

rum baba

7g dry yeast
¾ cup (110g) plain flour
2 tablespoons caster sugar
¼ cup (60ml) warm milk
2 eggs, beaten lightly
60g butter, melted
rum syrup
1½ cups (330g) caster sugar
1 cup (250ml) water
2 tablespoons dark rum

1 Preheat oven to 200°C/180°C fan-forced. Grease six ½ cup (125ml) moulds.
2 Cream yeast, 1 teaspoon of the flour, 1 teaspoon of the sugar and the milk in small bowl; cover, stand in warm place about 10 minutes or until mixture is frothy.
3 Sift remaining flour and remaining sugar into large bowl, stir in yeast mixture, egg and butter; beat about 3 minutes with wooden spoon until batter is smooth. Place batter in large greased bowl, cover; stand in warm place about 40 minutes or until batter has doubled in size.
4 Beat batter again. Divide batter among moulds; stand, uncovered, until batter rises three-quarters of the way up side of moulds. Place moulds on oven tray;.
5 Bake babas about 15 minutes; cover tops if beginning to darken too much. Turn babas onto wire rack over tray.
6 Make rum syrup; pour hot syrup over hot babas. Place babas on serving plates; pour syrup from tray over babas until all syrup has been absorbed.
rum syrup Stir sugar and water in saucepan over heat, without boiling, until sugar dissolves. Bring to the boil; boil, uncovered, without stirring, 2 minutes. Remove from heat; stir in rum.

prep + cook time 1 hour 30 minutes (+ standing) **serves** 6

golden syrup dumplings

1¼ cups (185g) self-raising flour
30g butter
⅓ cup (115g) golden syrup
⅓ cup (80ml) milk
sauce
30g butter
¾ cup (165g) firmly packed brown sugar
½ cup (175g) golden syrup
1⅔ cups (410ml) water

1 Sift flour into medium bowl; rub in butter. Gradually stir in golden syrup and milk.
2 Make sauce.
3 Drop rounded tablespoonfuls of mixture into simmering sauce; simmer, covered, about 20 minutes. Serve dumplings with sauce.
sauce Stir ingredients in medium saucepan over heat, without boiling, until sugar dissolves; bring to the boil, without stirring. Reduce heat; simmer, uncovered, 5 minutes.

prep + cook time 40 minutes **serves** 4

chocolate brownies with raspberry sauce

125g butter
1 cup (220g) firmly packed brown sugar
1 teaspoon vanilla extract
4 eggs
½ cup (75g) plain flour
½ cup (75g) self-raising flour
¾ cup (105g) chopped unroasted hazelnuts
200g dark eating chocolate, melted
200g white eating chocolate, melted
raspberry sauce
¾ cup (240g) raspberry jam
¼ cup (60ml) water
2 teaspoons cornflour
1 tablespoon water, extra

1 Preheat oven to 170°C/150°C fan-forced. Grease deep 20cm square cake pan; line base with baking paper.
2 Beat butter, sugar and extract in small bowl with electric mixer until light and fluffy. Beat in eggs one at a time; stir in sifted flour and nuts.
3 Divide mixture between two bowls. Stir dark chocolate into one bowl; spread into pan. Stir white chocolate into remaining bowl; spread over dark chocolate mixture.
4 Bake brownie about 1 hour or until golden brown.
5 Make raspberry sauce.
6 Turn brownie onto serving plate, serve hot with sauce; dust with sifted icing sugar, if you like.
raspberry sauce Stir jam and water in small saucepan over heat until jam is melted. Stir in blended cornflour and extra water, over high heat until sauce boils and thickens.

prep + cook time 1 hour 15 minutes **serves** 6
tips Brownies are best made close to serving time. Sauce can be made a day ahead; keep, covered, in refrigerator.

individual tiramisu

1 teaspoon white sugar
2 teaspoons instant coffee granules
1 teaspoon cocoa powder, sifted
⅔ cup (160ml) boiling water
250g cream cheese, softened
300ml cream
¾ cup (120g) icing sugar
6 sponge finger biscuits (90g)
2 teaspoons cocoa powder, extra

1 Blend white sugar, coffee and cocoa with the water in small bowl; cool.
2 Beat cheese in small bowl with electric mixer until smooth. Add cream and icing sugar; beat until smooth.
3 Halve biscuits crossways; dip in coffee mixture. Divide half the biscuits among four 1¼ cup (310ml) glasses. Divide half the cream mixture among glasses; top with remaining biscuits then remaining cream mixture. Refrigerate 30 minutes. Serve dusted with sifted extra cocoa powder.

prep time 20 minutes (+ refrigeration) **serves** 4

orange blossom cakes

100g butter, softened
1 teaspoon orange blossom water
½ cup (110g) caster sugar
2 eggs
1 cup (150g) self-raising flour
¼ cup (30g) almond meal
½ cup (125ml) milk
orange blossom glacé icing
1 cup (160g) icing sugar
10g softened butter
1 teaspoon orange blossom water
1 tablespoon water, approximately

1 Preheat oven to 180°C/160°C fan-forced. Grease six-hole (¾ cup/ 180ml) mini fluted tube pan or texas muffin pan.
2 Beat butter, blossom water and sugar in small bowl with electric mixer until light and fluffy. Beat in eggs, one at a time (mixture will curdle). Stir in sifted flour, meal and milk, in two batches.
3 Divide mixture between pan holes; bake about 25 minutes. Stand cakes in pan 5 minutes before turning, top-side up, onto wire rack to cool.
4 Meanwhile, make orange blossom glacé icing. Drizzle icing over cakes.
orange blossom glacé icing Sift icing sugar into small heatproof bowl; stir in butter, blossom water and enough of the boiling water to make a firm paste. Stir over small saucepan of simmering water until icing is pourable.

prep + cook time 45 minutes **makes** 6
tip Orange blossom water is a concentrated flavouring made from orange blossoms; it is available from Middle-Eastern food stores, some supermarkets and delicatessens. Citrus flavourings are very different.

flourless chocolate cakes with latte sauce

150g dark eating chocolate, chopped coarsely
150g butter, chopped coarsely
4 eggs, separated
1 cup (220g) firmly packed brown sugar
1¼ cups (150g) ground almonds
latte sauce
180g white eating chocolate, chopped coarsely
½ cup (125ml) cream
2 tablespoons coffee-flavoured liqueur
1 teaspoon instant coffee granules

1 Preheat oven to 180°C/160°C fan-forced. Grease 12-hole (⅓ cup/80ml) muffin pan.
2 Make latte sauce.
3 Stir chocolate and butter in medium saucepan over low heat until smooth. Cool 5 minutes. Stir in egg yolks, sugar and ground almonds. Transfer mixture to large bowl.
4 Beat egg whites in small bowl with electric mixer until soft peaks form; fold into chocolate mixture, in two batches.
5 Divide mixture between pan holes; bake cakes about 25 minutes. Cool cakes in pan 5 minutes before turning, top-side down, onto serving plates. Serve warm cakes drizzled with latte sauce.
latte sauce Stir ingredients in small saucepan over low heat until smooth. Cool about 30 minutes or until thickened slightly.

prep + cook time 45 minutes (+ cooling) **makes** 12
tip You may need to run a spatula carefully around the edges of the cakes to loosen them before turning out of the pan.

raspberry brownie ice-cream cake

1 litre vanilla ice-cream, softened
150g frozen raspberries
125g butter, chopped coarsely
200g dark eating chocolate, chopped coarsely
½ cup (110g) caster sugar
2 eggs
1¼ cups (185g) plain flour
150g milk eating chocolate, chopped coarsely
1 tablespoon icing sugar

1 Line deep 23cm-round cake pan with plastic wrap, extending wrap so it will cover pan. Combine ice-cream and raspberries in medium bowl. Spoon ice-cream into pan; smooth surface. Fold plastic wrap over to enclose. Freeze 3 hours or until firm.
2 Preheat oven to 160°C/140°C fan-forced. Remove ice-cream from pan, still wrapped in plastic; place on tray. Return to freezer.
3 Grease same pan; line base and side with baking paper.
4 Stir butter, dark chocolate and sugar in medium saucepan over low heat until smooth. Cool 10 minutes.
5 Stir in eggs, sifted flour and milk chocolate. Spread mixture into pan.
6 Bake brownie about 30 minutes; cool in pan.
7 Split brownie in half. Sandwich ice-cream cake between brownie slices; serve immediately, dusted with sifted icing sugar. Serve with fresh raspberries, if you like.

prep + cook time 1 hour (+ freezing) **serves** 12

rum and raisin chocolate cake

¼ cup (60ml) dark rum
1 cup (180g) raisins, chopped finely
300g dark eating chocolate, chopped coarsely
150g butter, chopped coarsely
⅔ cup (150g) firmly packed brown sugar
⅔ cup (100g) self-raising flour
2 tablespoons cocoa powder
3 eggs, separated
2 teaspoons cocoa powder, extra

1 Preheat oven to 180°C/160°C fan-forced. Grease deep 23cm-round cake pan; line base and side with baking paper.
2 Warm rum in small saucepan, add raisins; stand 1 hour.
3 Stir chocolate and butter in small saucepan over low heat until smooth. Transfer to large bowl; cool 5 minutes. Stir in sugar, sifted flour and cocoa, egg yolks and raisin mixture.
4 Beat egg whites in small bowl with electric mixer until soft peaks form; fold into chocolate mixture, in two batches. Pour mixture into pan.
5 Bake cake about 1 hour. Stand cake in pan 15 minutes before turning, top-side up, onto serving plate. Serve cake warm or cold dusted with extra sifted cocoa. Serve cake with whipped cream, if you like.

prep + cook time 1 hour 15 minutes (+ standing) **serves** 12

lemon ricotta cheesecake

250g ginger nut biscuits
125g butter, melted
filling
3 teaspoons gelatine
¼ cup (60ml) water
250g cream cheese
750g ricotta cheese
1 tablespoon finely grated lemon rind
½ cup (110g) caster sugar
⅓ cup (80ml) lemon juice
300ml thickened cream, whipped
passionfruit topping
½ cup (125ml) orange juice
2 tablespoons passionfruit pulp
1 tablespoon caster sugar
2 teaspoons gelatine

1 Process biscuits until fine. Add butter, process until combined. Press mixture over base of 26cm springform tin. Refrigerate 30 minutes.
2 Make filling by sprinkling gelatine over the water in small heatproof jug; stand jug in small saucepan of simmering water. Stir until gelatine dissolves; cool 5 minutes.
3 Beat cheeses, rind, sugar and juice in large bowl with electric mixer until smooth. Stir in gelatine mixture; fold in cream. Spread filling into tin; refrigerate overnight.
4 Make passionfruit topping.
5 Pour topping over cheesecake. Refrigerate until set.
passionfruit topping Stir juice, passionfruit and sugar in small saucepan over low heat until sugar is dissolved. Remove from heat; add gelatine, stir until dissolved. Cool 15 minutes.

prep + cook time 30 minutes (+ cooling and refrigeration) **serves** 16

sticky banana macadamia pudding with butterscotch sauce

2 cups (300g) self-raising flour
½ teaspoon bicarbonate of soda
1 teaspoon mixed spice
150g butter, softened
1 cup (200g) firmly packed
  brown sugar
3 eggs
1½ cups mashed overripe banana
⅓ cup (80g) sour cream
⅓ cup (80ml) milk
½ cup (70g) coarsely chopped
  roasted macadamias
2 tablespoons finely chopped
  glacé ginger

butterscotch sauce
1 cup (200g) firmly packed
  brown sugar
1 cup (250ml) thickened cream
125g butter, chopped

1 Preheat oven to 180°C/160°C fan-forced. Grease a deep 22cm-round cake pan; line base and side with baking paper.
2 Sift flour, soda and spice into medium bowl.
3 Beat butter and sugar in small bowl with electric mixer until well combined. Beat in eggs, one at a time. Transfer mixture to large bowl; stir in half the flour mixture, half of the banana then sour cream and milk. Stir in remaining flour and banana, then nuts and glacé ginger. Spread mixture into pan.
4 Bake pudding about 1 hour 10 minutes or until cooked when tested. Stand in pan 10 minutes before turning onto wire rack to cool.
5 Meanwhile, make butterscotch sauce.
6 Serve warm pudding with sauce and cream.
butterscotch sauce Stir ingredients in medium saucepan over heat, without boiling, until sugar has dissolved. Simmer, stirring, 3 minutes.

prep + cook time 1 hour 30 minutes (+ standing) **serves** 8
tip You will need 3 large overripe bananas (690g) for this recipe.

385

glossary

allspice also known as pimento or jamaican pepper; is so named because it tastes like a combination of nutmeg, cumin, cinnamon and clove. It is available whole or ground, from most supermarkets and specialty spice stores.

almonds

blanched almonds with brown skins removed.

flaked paper-thin slices.

meal also known as ground almonds; nuts are powdered to a coarse flour texture.

slivered small pieces cut lengthways.

vienna toffee-coated almonds.

baking powder a raising agent consisting mainly of two parts cream of tartar to one part bicarbonate of soda (baking soda).

bicarbonate of soda also known as baking soda; a mild alkali used as a leavening agent in baking.

biscuits, butternut snap crunchy biscuit made from rolled oats, coconut and golden syrup.

breadcrumbs

fresh bread, usually white, processed into crumbs.

stale crumbs made by grating, blending or processing 1- or 2-day-old bread.

brioche Rich egg-and-butter brioche can be made in the shape of a loaf or roll, but the most recognisable variation is perhaps the "brioche a tete", 'a roll with a head', formed by placing a small ball of dough on top of a larger one. Eaten freshly baked or toasted; available from cake or specialty bread shops.

butter we use salted butter unless stated; 125g is equal to 1 stick (4 ounces). Unsalted or "sweet" butter has no salt added and is perhaps the most popular among pastry chefs.

buttermilk in spite of its name, buttermilk is actually low in fat. Originally the term given to the slightly sour liquid left after butter was churned from cream, today it is intentionally made from no-fat or low-fat milk with specific bacterial cultures added during manufacturing. It is readily available from the dairy department in supermarkets.

cardamom a spice native to India and used extensively in its cuisine; can be purchased in pod, seed or ground form. Has a distinctive aromatic, sweetly rich flavour and is one of the world's most expensive spices. Used to flavour curries, rice dishes, sweet desserts and cakes.

cashews plump, kidney-shaped, golden-brown nuts with a distinctive sweet, buttery flavour and containing about 48% fat. Due to their high fat content they should be stored in the refrigerator to avoid becoming rancid.

cheese

cream commonly known as philadelphia or philly; a soft cow-milk cheese with a fat content of 14–33%.

mascarpone an Italian fresh cultured-cream product made in much the same way as yogurt. Whiteish to creamy yellow in colour, with a buttery-rich, luscious texture. Soft, creamy and spreadable, it is used in many Italian desserts and as an accompaniment to a dessert of fresh fruit.

ricotta a soft, sweet, moist, white cow-milk cheese with a low fat content (about 8.5%) and a slightly grainy texture. The name roughly translates as "cooked again" and refers to ricotta's manufacture from a whey that is itself a by-product of other cheese making.

cherry ripe bar dark chocolate bar made with coconut and cherries; standard size bar weighs 55g.

chocolate

Choc Bits also known as chocolate chips or chocolate morsels; available in milk, white and dark chocolate. Made of cocoa liquor, cocoa butter, sugar and an emulsifier, these hold their shape in baking and are ideal for decorating.

dark eating also called semi-sweet or luxury chocolate; made of a high percentage of cocoa liquor and cocoa butter, and little added sugar. Unless stated otherwise, we use dark eating chocolate in this book as it's ideal for use in desserts and cakes.

Melts small discs of compounded milk, white or dark chocolate ideal for melting and moulding.

milk most popular eating chocolate, mild and very sweet; similar in make-up to dark with the difference being the addition of milk solids.

white eating contains no cocoa solids but derives its sweet flavour from cocoa butter. Very sensitive to heat.

chocolate hazelnut spread also known as Nutella; made of cocoa powder, hazelnuts, sugar and milk.

cinnamon available both in the piece (called sticks or quills) and ground into powder; one of the world's most common spices, used universally as a sweet, fragrant flavouring for both sweet and savoury foods. The dried inner bark of the shoots of the Sri Lankan native cinnamon tree; much of what is sold as the real thing is in fact cassia, Chinese cinnamon, from the bark of the cassia tree. Less expensive to process than true cinnamon, it is often blended with Sri Lankan cinnamon to produce the type of "cinnamon" most commonly found in supermarkets.

cloves dried flower buds of a tropical tree; can be used whole or in ground form. They have a strong scent and taste so should be used sparingly.

cocoa powder also known as unsweetened cocoa; cocoa beans (cacao seeds) that have been fermented, roasted, shelled, ground into powder then cleared of most of the fat content.

coconut

cream obtained commercially from the first pressing of the coconut flesh alone,

without the addition of water; the second pressing (less rich) is sold as coconut milk. Available in cans and cartons at most supermarkets.

desiccated concentrated, dried, unsweetened and finely shredded coconut flesh.

flaked dried flaked coconut flesh.

milk not the liquid found inside the fruit (coconut water) but the diluted liquid from the second pressing of the white flesh of a mature coconut. Available in cans and cartons at most supermarkets.

shredded unsweetened thin strips of dried coconut flesh.

cornflakes commercially manufactured cereal made of dehydrated then baked crisp flakes of corn. Also available is a prepared finely ground mixture used for coating or crumbing food before frying or baking, sold as "crushed corn flakes" in 300g packages in most supermarkets.

cornflour also known as cornstarch. Available made from corn or wheat (wheaten cornflour, gluten-free, gives a lighter texture in cakes).

cream we use fresh pouring cream, also known as pure cream. It has no additives, and contains a minimum fat content of 35%.

thickened a whipping cream that contains a thickener (minimum fat content of 35%).

cream of tartar the acid ingredient in baking powder; added to confectionery mixtures to help prevent sugar from crystallising. Keeps frostings creamy and improves volume when beating egg whites.

cumquat orange-coloured citrus fruit about the size of walnuts. Usually preserved or used for making jam, the skin is always retained.

custard powder instant mixture used to make pouring custard; similar to North American instant pudding mixes.

dates fruit of the date palm tree, eaten fresh or dried, on their own or in prepared dishes. About 4cm to 6cm in length, oval and plump, thin-skinned, with a honey-sweet flavour and sticky texture. Best known, perhaps, for their inclusion in sticky toffee pudding; also found in muesli; muffins, scones and cakes; compotes and stewed fruit desserts.

dried currants tiny, almost black raisins so-named after a grape variety that originated in Corinth, Greece. These are not the same as fresh currants, which are the fruit of a plant in the gooseberry family.

eggs we use large chicken eggs weighing an average of 60g unless stated otherwise. If a recipe calls for raw or barely cooked eggs, exercise caution if there is a salmonella problem in your area, particularly in food eaten by children and pregnant women.

figs originally from the countries that border the eastern Mediterranean; are best eaten in peak season, at the height of summer. Vary in skin and flesh colour according to type not ripeness: the purple-black mission or black mission fig, with pink flesh, is a rich-flavoured, good all-rounder; the thick-skinned, pale green kadota, another all-purpose fruit, is good canned or dried as well as fresh; the yellow smyrna has nutty-tasting flesh; and the pale olive, golden-skinned adriatic has honey-sweet, light pink flesh. When ripe, figs should be unblemished and bursting with flesh; nectar beads at the base indicate when a fig is at its best. Figs are also glacéd (candied), dried or canned in sugar syrup; these are usually sold at health-food stores, Middle Eastern food shops or specialty cheese counters.

flour

plain also known as all-purpose; unbleached wheat flour is the best for baking: the gluten content ensures a strong dough, which produces a light result.

rice very fine, almost powdery, gluten-free flour; made from ground white rice. Used in baking, as a thickener, and in some Asian noodles and desserts.

self-raising all-purpose plain or wholemeal flour with baking powder and salt added; can be made at home with plain or wholemeal flour sifted with baking powder in the proportion of 1 cup flour to 2 teaspoons baking powder.

wholemeal also known as wholewheat flour; milled with the wheat germ so is higher in fibre and more nutritional than plain flour.

food colouring vegetable-based substance available in liquid, paste or gel form.

gelatine we use dried (powdered) gelatine in the recipes in this book; it's also available in sheet form known as leaf gelatine. A thickening agent made from either collagen, a protein found in animal connective tissue and bones, or certain algae (agar-agar). Three teaspoons of dried gelatine (8g or one sachet) is roughly equivalent to four gelatine leaves. Professionals use leaf gelatine because it generally results in a smoother, clearer consistency; it is also most commonly used throughout Europe. The two types are interchangable but leaf gelatine gives a much clearer mixture than dried gelatine; it's perfect in dishes where appearance really counts.

ginger

fresh also called green or root ginger; the thick gnarled root of a tropical plant. Store, peeled, covered with dry sherry in a jar and refrigerated, or frozen in an airtight container.

glacé fresh ginger root preserved in sugar syrup; crystallised ginger (sweetened with cane sugar) can be substituted if rinsed with warm water and dried before using.

ground also known as powdered ginger; used as a flavouring in baking but cannot be substituted for fresh.

glacé fruit fruit such as pineapple, apricots, peaches and pears that are cooked in a heavy sugar syrup then dried.

golden syrup a by-product of refined sugarcane; pure maple syrup or honey can be substituted.

green ginger wine beverage 14% alcohol by volume, has the taste of fresh ginger. In cooking, substitute dry (white) vermouth if you prefer.

grenadine a non-alcoholic syrup made from pomegranate juice; bright red in colour, it's used to colour and flavour drinks and desserts.

hazelnuts also known as filberts; plump, grape-sized, rich, sweet nut with a brown skin that is removed by rubbing heated nuts together vigorously in a tea-towel.

meal is made by grounding the hazelnuts to a coarse flour texture for use in baking or as a thickening agent.

jelly crystals a combination of sugar, gelatine, colours and flavours; when dissolved in water, the solution sets as firm jelly.

jersey caramels confectionery made from sugar, glucose, condensed milk, flour, oil and gelatine.

liqueur

almond-flavoured such as amaretto.

cherry-flavoured such as kirsch.

chocolate-flavoured such as crème de cacao.

coconut-flavoured such as Malibu.

coffee-flavoured such as Tia Maria or Kahlua.

hazelnut-flavoured such as Frangelico.

irish cream we used Baileys Irish Cream, a smooth and creamy natural blend of fresh Irish cream, the finest Irish spirits, Irish whisky, cocoa and vanilla.

orange-flavoured you could use cointreau, grand marnier or curaçao.

macadamias native to Australia; fairly large, slightly soft, buttery rich nut. Used to make oil and macadamia butter; equally good in salads or cakes and pastries; delicious eaten on their own. Should always be stored in the fridge to prevent their high oil content turning them rancid.

maple-flavoured syrup is made from sugar cane and is also known as golden or pancake syrup. It is not a substitute for pure maple syrup.

maple syrup distilled from the sap of sugar maple trees found only in Canada and about ten states in the USA. Most often eaten with pancakes or waffles, but also used as an ingredient in baking or in preparing desserts. Maple-flavoured syrup or pancake syrup is not an adequate substitute for the real thing.

marmalade a preserve, usually based on citrus fruit and its rind, cooked with sugar until the mixture has an intense flavour and thick consistency. Orange, lemon and lime are some of the commercially prepared varieties available.

marsala a fortified Italian wine produced in the region surrounding the Sicilian city of Marsala; recognisable by its intense amber colour and complex aroma. Often used in cooking, especially in sauces, risottos and desserts.

milk we use full-cream homogenised milk unless otherwise specified.

caramel top 'n' fill a canned milk product made of condensed milk that has been boiled to a caramel.

sweetened condensed a canned milk product consisting of milk with more than half the water content removed and sugar added to the remaining milk.

mixed dried fruit a combination of sultanas, raisins, currants, mixed peel and cherries.

mixed spice a classic mixture generally containing caraway, allspice, coriander, cumin, nutmeg and ginger, although cinnamon and other spices can be added. It is used with fruit and in cakes.

nutmeg a strong and pungent spice ground from the dried nut of an evergreen tree native to Indonesia. Usually found ground but the flavour is more intense from a whole nut, available from spice shops, so it's best to grate your own. Used most often in baking and milk-based desserts, but also works nicely in savoury dishes. Found in mixed spice mixtures.

oil, vegetable any of a number of oils sourced from plant rather than animal fats.

orange blossom water is a concentrated flavouring made from orange blossoms; it is available from Middle-Eastern food stores, some supermarkets and delicatessens. Citrus flavourings are very different.

pecans native to the US and now grown locally; pecans are golden brown, buttery and rich. Good in savoury as well as sweet dishes; walnuts are a good substitute.

pepitas are the pale green kernels of dried pumpkin seeds; they can be bought plain or salted.

poppy seeds small, dried, bluish-grey seeds of the poppy plant, with a crunchy texture and nutty flavour. Can be purchased whole or ground in most supermarkets.

quince yellow-skinned fruit with hard texture and astringent, tart taste; eaten cooked or as a preserve. Long, slow cooking makes the flesh a deep rose pink.

rhubarb actually a vegetable, rhubarb is a member of the buckwheat family. It has an intensely tart flavour which makes it a good dessert and pie filling when sweetened and combined with other fruit.

roasting/toasting
nuts and dried coconut can be roasted in the oven to restore their fresh flavour and release their aromatic essential oils. Spread them evenly onto an oven tray then roast in a moderate oven for about 5 minutes. Desiccated coconut, pine nuts and sesame seeds roast more evenly if stirred over low heat in a heavy-based frying pan; their natural oils will help turn them golden brown.

rolled oats flattened oat grain rolled into flakes and traditionally used for porridge. Instant oats are also available, but traditional oats are best for baking.

rosewater extract made from crushed rose petals, called gulab in India; used for its aromatic quality in many sweetmeats and desserts.

rum we use a dark underproof rum (not overproof) for a more subtle flavour in cooking. White rum is almost colourless, sweet and used mostly in drinks.

sago a grain often used in puddings and desserts; similar to tapioca but sourced from a variety of palm, while tapioca is from the root of the cassava plant.

semolina coarsely ground flour milled from durum wheat; the flour used in making gnocchi, pasta and couscous.

sponge finger biscuits also known as savoiardi, savoy biscuits or lady's fingers, they are Italian-style crisp fingers made from sponge cake mixture.

star anise a dried star-shaped pod whose seeds have an astringent aniseed flavour; commonly used to flavour stocks and marinades.

sugar

brown a soft, finely granulated sugar retaining molasses for its characteristic colour and flavour.

caster also known as superfine or finely granulated table sugar.

demerara small-grained golden-coloured crystal sugar.

icing also known as confectioners' sugar or powdered sugar; pulverised granulated sugar crushed together with a small amount of cornflour.

pure icing also known as confectioners' sugar or powdered sugar.

sunflower seeds grey-green, slightly soft, oily kernels; a nutritious snack.

tangelo a cross between a grapefruit and a tangerine, it's eaten like an orange.

vanilla

bean dried, long, thin pod from a tropical golden orchid grown in central and South America and Tahiti; the minuscule black seeds inside the bean are used to impart a luscious vanilla flavour in baking and desserts.

extract obtained from vanilla beans infused in water; a non-alcoholic version of essence.

vinegar, malt made from fermented malt and beech shavings.

walnuts as well as being a good source of fibre and healthy oils, nuts contain a range of vitamins, minerals and other beneficial plant components called phytochemicals. Each type of nut has a special make-up and walnuts contain the beneficial omega-3 fatty acids, which is terrific news for people who dislike the taste of fish.

yeast (dried and fresh), a raising agent. Granular (7g sachets) and fresh compressed (20g blocks) yeast can almost always be substituted one for the other.

yogurt we use plain full-cream yogurt.

index

A
almond and raspberry
  frozen pudding 13
apples
  apple and fig bread
    pudding 45
  apple and marmalade
    streusel pudding 14
  apple and pear
    crumble 82
  apple charlotte 69
  fresh apple
    soufflés 299
  warm apple cake with
    brandy butterscotch
    sauce 326
apricot and honey
  soufflés 296
apricot upside down
  cakes 350

B
bananas
  banana caramel
    bread and butter
    pudding 125
  banana caramel
    puddings 46
  banana macadamia
    pudding, sticky,
    with butterscotch
    sauce 385
  banana pudding with
    espresso syrup 42
berries
  berry and hazelnut
    crumble 86
  berry coconut and
    yogurt parfaits 49
  berry compote 133
  berry mousse 225
  berry mousse
    cake 222
  mixed berry sauce 252
bitter orange sauce 106
black forest soufflés
  287

black forest upside
  down puddings 33
blackberry soufflés 312
blueberry cake with
  vanilla syrup 357
blueberry crumble 81
brandy butterscotch
  sauce 326
brandy cream 178
bread and butter
  pudding 114
  banana caramel 125
  chocolate 117
  heavenly 121
butterscotch sauce 22,
  25, 185, 321, 346, 385

C
cakes see also
  dessert cakes
  berry mousse 222
  choc fruit cake,
    frozen 113
  chocolate espresso
    mousse 206
  chocolate mousse
    cake with coffee
    anglaise 197
  irish cream and
    dark choc mousse
    cake 210
  sponge 41
caramel sauce 259
caramel soufflés with
  walnut praline 288
cardamom orange
  mousse cakes 338
charlotte
  apple 69
  pear, with fig syrup 66
cherry filling 287
chocolate see also
  white chocolate
  choc fruit cake,
    frozen 113
  chocolate and
    berry trifle 54

(chocolate continued)
  chocolate and golden
    syrup pudding,
    steamed 185
  chocolate bread
    and butter 117
  chocolate bread
    pudding with
    brandy cream 178
  chocolate brownies
    with raspberry
    sauce 370
  chocolate cherry
    meringue desserts 70
  chocolate chip
    pudding 182
  chocolate custard,
    baked 158
  chocolate espresso
    mousse cake 206
  chocolate fondants
    341
  chocolate hazelnut
    self-saucing
    puddings 264
  chocolate hazelnut
    steamed pudding 186
  chocolate liqueur
    soufflés 283
  chocolate mocha
    dacquoise terrine 353
  chocolate mousse
    194, 217
  chocolate mousse
    cake with coffee
    anglaise 197
  chocolate mousse
    puffs 205
  chocolate nut bavarois
    with raspberry
    sauce 201
  chocolate, pear and
    hazelnut self-saucing
    pudding 248
  chocolate pecan
    pudding 101

(*chocolate* continued)
chocolate pudding
  cake 358
chocolate sauce 182
chocolate self-saucing
  pudding 256
chocolate soufflé 276
chocolate sticky
  date pudding 22
chocolate
  zabaglione 245
dark chocolate and
  almond torte 329
dark chocolate
  ganache 329
double chocolate
  mousse 198
flourless chocolate
  cakes with latte
  sauce 377
frozen chocolate
  and coconut
  soufflés 280
hot chocolate
  soufflés with
  liqueur cream 279
irish cream and
  dark choc mousse
  cake 210
microwave choc-cherry
  self-saucing
  pudding 263
milk chocolate
  mousse 198
milk chocolate rum and
  raisin mousse 209
rum and raisin
  chocolate cake 381
christmas pudding
  classic boiled 10
  steamed 170
  white chocolate
  frozen 110
cinnamon custard,
  quick 69
cinnamon flan 157

citrus almond syrup
  cake 325
citrus rice pudding 134
citrus sauce 121
clafoutis
  plum 26
  summer berry 65
clove panna cotta
  with fresh figs 129
coconut
  coco-cherry ice-cream
  timbale 109
  coconut bread
  pudding 122
  coconut crumble 82
  coconut rice
  puddings 137
coffee
  coffee and pecan
  puddings with
  caramel sauce 97
  coffee anglaise 197
  coffee caramel
  cakes 337
  coffee cream 186
  coffee mousse 217
  coffee soufflés
  with pecan praline
  cream 300
college pudding 173
cream cheese
  frosting 333
creamed rice 142
creamy marsala
  soufflés 291
crème anglaise 322
crème brûlée 145
  passionfruit and
  coconut 146
  passionfruit and
  lime 149
crème caramel 154
  coffee 150
  ginger 153
crumble
  apple and pear 82
  berry and hazelnut 86

(*crumble* continued)
blueberry 81
coconut 82
mocha 77
muesli 82
pear and plum
  amaretti 93
rhubarb and apple 90
topping 74, 82, 90, 354
cumquat and almond
  dessert cake 322
cumquat jam pudding
  with custard cream 34
curd, passionfruit 334
custard 101, 118,
  121, 165
custard, baked 162
custard cream 34
custard sauce 33
D
date and butterscotch
  self-saucing
  pudding 259
date pudding,
  steamed 190
dessert cakes
  see also cakes
  apricot upside down
  350
  blueberry cake with
  vanilla syrup 357
  cardamom orange
  mousse 338
  chocolate brownies
  with raspberry
  sauce 370
  chocolate fondants 341
  chocolate mocha
  dacquoise terrine
  353
  chocolate pudding 358
  citrus almond
  syrup 325
  coffee caramel 337
  cumquat and
  almond 322

(*dessert cakes*
continued)
dark chocolate and
  almond torte 329
fig and almond cake
  with butterscotch
  sauce 321
flourless chocolate
  cakes with latte
  sauce 377
golden syrup
  dumplings 369
hummingbird 333
individual tiramisu 373
irish pudding 365
lemon ricotta
  cheesecake 382
maple pecan 349
moist whole
  orange 330
orange and date
  dessert muffins 361
orange blossom 374
passionfruit sponge
  roll 334
pear crumble 354
raspberry brownie
  ice-cream 378
raspberry hazelnut 362
rum and raisin
  chocolate 381
rum baba 366
semolina and yogurt
  lemon-syrup 345
sticky banana
  macadamia pudding
  with butterscotch
  sauce 385
sticky date roll
  with butterscotch
  sauce 346
upside down toffee
  date and banana 342
warm apple cake with
  brandy butterscotch
  sauce 326

E
espresso syrup 42
F
fig and almond cake
  with butterscotch
  sauce 321
fig and brioche
  pudding 29
fluffy fruit mousse 241
frozen puddings
  almond and
    raspberry 13
  glacé fruit and
    citrus 106
fruit and nut puddings
  almond and raspberry
    frozen 12
  apple and fig bread 45
  apple and marmalade
    streusel 14
  apple and pear
    crumble 82
  apple charlotte 69
  banana caramel 46
  banana pudding with
    espresso syrup 42
  berry and hazelnut
    crumble 86
  berry coconut and
    yogurt parfaits 49
  black forest
    upside down 33
  blueberry crumble 81
  chocolate and
    berry trifle 54
  chocolate cherry
    meringue desserts 70
  chocolate pecan 101
  chocolate sticky
    date 22
  classic boiled
    christmas 10
  classic trifle 53
  coffee and pecan
    puddings with
    caramel sauce 97

(*fruit and nut puddings*
continued)
  creamy lemon crumble
    74
  cumquat jam pudding
    with custard cream
    34
  fig and brioche 29
  ginger sticky date 25
  glacé fruit puddings
    with ginger syrup 85
  hazelnut tiramisu 98
  lemon curd,
    blueberry and
    meringue trifle 50
  lemon meringue 18
  lime coconut bake 73
  mango and lemon
    chiffon trifle 62
  mocha pear crumble 77
  peach and raspberry
    meringue roll 94
  peach and
    raspberry trifle 61
  pear and plum
    amaretti crumble 93
  pear charlottes with
    fig syrup 66
  pecan dumplings in
    honey syrup 102
  pineapple crunch 89
  plum clafoutis 26
  plum cobbler 78
  quince sponge 30
  raspberry and
    chocolate mousse
    trifle 58
  rhubarb and apple
    crumble 90
  rhubarb and pear
    sponge 38
  rhubarb and strawberry
    sponge 41
  sago plum puddings
    with orange cream
    37

(*fruit and nut puddings*
continued)
summer 17
summer berry
clafoutis 65
toffee date and
ginger 21
tropical fruit trifle 57
fruit mince and brioche
pudding 165
fudge sauce 248
G
ganache, dark
chocolate 329
ginger
ginger and orange
self-saucing
pudding 268
ginger butterscotch
sauce 21
ginger crème
caramels 153
ginger pudding,
steamed 174
ginger sauce 233
ginger sticky date
pudding 25
ginger syrup 85
soufflés 304
glacé fruit and citrus
frozen puddings 106
glacé fruit puddings
with ginger syrup 85
glacé ginger and
peach mousse 233
golden syrup
dumplings 369
grapefruit, pink,
soufflés 316
H
hazelnut butterscotch
self-saucing
pudding 271
hazelnut tiramisu 98
heavenly bread and
butter puddings 121

honey lime bavarois 229
honey mousse 226
honey syrup 102
hummingbird cake 333
I
irish cream and
dark choc mousse
cake 210
irish pudding cake 365
J
jaffa self-saucing
pudding 255
L
latte sauce 377
lemon
lemon and mixed
berry self-saucing
pudding 252
lemon chiffon 62
lemon crumble,
creamy 74
lemon curd, blueberry
and meringue
trifle 50
lemon delicious
pudding 251
lemon meringue
pudding 18
lemon ricotta
cheesecake 382
lemon soufflés,
tangy 308
lemon syrup 345
lime coconut bake 73
lime syrup 325
liqueur cream 279
M
mango
mango and lemon
chiffon trifle 62
mango and lime
mousse 242
mango creams 230
mango soufflés
with chocolate
collars 295

maple butterscotch
sauce 349
maple pecan cake 349
margarita mousse 218
marsala soufflés,
creamy 291
mascarpone cream 362
meringue 70
topping 18
milk chocolate
mousse 198
milk chocolate rum
and raisin 209
milk puddings
baked chocolate
custard 158
baked rice custard 141
banana caramel
bread and butter
pudding 125
bread and butter
pudding 114
chocolate bread
and butter 117
cinnamon flan 157
citrus rice pudding 134
clove panna cotta
with fresh figs 129
coco-cherry ice-cream
timbale 109
coconut bread
pudding 122
coconut rice
puddings 137
coffee crème
caramels 150
creamed rice 142
crème brûlée 145
crème caramel 154
custard, baked 162
frozen choc fruit
cake 113
fruit mince and
brioche pudding 165
ginger crème
caramels 153

(*milk puddings* continued)
glacé fruit and citrus frozen 106
heavenly bread and butter 121
nougat almond custard 161
passionfruit and coconut crème brûlée 146
passionfruit and lime crème brûlée 149
passionfruit panna cotta with mango 130
queen of puddings 166
vanilla panna cotta with berry compote 133
white choc and raspberry croissant 118
white chocolate and black cherry creamed rice 138
white chocolate frozen christmas 110
white chocolate panna cotta with passionfruit sauce 126
mocha bavarian with pecan praline 213
mocha butter cream 353
mocha mousse frozen 214
marbled 217
mocha, pear and nut self-saucing pudding 260
mocha pear crumble 77
mousses
berry 225
berry mousse cake 222
chocolate 194

(*mousses* continued)
chocolate espresso mousse cake 206
chocolate mousse cake with coffee anglaise 197
chocolate mousse puffs 205
chocolate nut bavarois with raspberry sauce 201
chocolate zabaglione 245
double chocolate 198
fluffy fruit 241
fresh raspberry 221
frozen mocha 214
glacé ginger and peach 233
honey lime bavarois 229
honey 226
irish cream and dark choc mousse cake 210
mango and lime 242
mango creams 230
marbled mocha 217
margarita 218
milk chocolate 198
milk chocolate rum and raisin 209
mocha bavarian with pecan praline 213
orange 338
piña colada 234
rockmelon passionfruit mousse 238
spicy pumpkin and hazelnut 237
white chocolate 202
muesli crumble 82
muffins, orange and date dessert 361

N
nougat almond custard 161

O
orange
moist whole orange cake 330
orange and date dessert muffins 361
orange and raspberry self-saucing pudding 272
orange blossom cakes 374
orange blossom glacé icing 374
orange cream 37
orange liqueur soufflés with macerated fruits 307
orange mousse 338
orange sauce 361
orange syrup 189, 338

P
panna cotta
clove, with fresh figs 129
passionfruit, with mango 130
vanilla, with berry compote 133
white chocolate with passionfruit sauce 126
passionfruit
hot passionfruit soufflé with raspberry cream 315
passionfruit and coconut crème brûlée 146
passionfruit and lime crème brûlée 149
passionfruit panna cotta with mango 130
passionfruit soufflés 284
passionfruit sponge roll 334
passionfruit topping 382

peach and raspberry
  meringue roll 94
peach and raspberry
  trifle 61
pear and plum amaretti
  crumble 93
pear charlottes with
  fig syrup 66
pear crumble cake 354
pear, red wine and
  honey soufflés 303
pecan dumplings in
  honey syrup 102
pecan praline 213
pecan praline cream 300
piña colada mousse 234
pineapple crunch 89
pineapple self-saucing
  pudding 267
pink grapefruit
  soufflés 316
plum clafoutis 26
plum cobbler 78
pumpkin and hazelnut
  mousse, spicy 237
pumpkin and maple
  pudding, steamed 181

Q
queen of puddings 166
quince and spice
  steamed pudding with
  orange syrup 189
quince sponge
  pudding 30

R
raspberries
  fresh raspberry
    mousse 221
  raspberry and
    chocolate mousse 58
  raspberry brownie
    ice-cream cake 378
  raspberry cream 315
  raspberry hazelnut
    cake 362
  raspberry mousse 222

(*raspberries* continued)
  raspberry sauce
    201, 370
  raspberry soufflés,
    hot 311
rhubarb
  rhubarb and apple
    crumble 90
  rhubarb and pear
    sponge pudding 38
  rhubarb and
    strawberry sponge
    pudding 41
rice, creamed 142
rice custard, baked 141
rice pudding
  citrus 134
  coconut 137
rockmelon passionfruit
  mousse 238
rosewater soufflés 292
rum and raisin
  chocolate cake 381
rum baba 366
rum syrup 366

S
sago plum puddings
  with orange cream 37
sauce
  bitter orange 106
  brandy butterscotch
    326
  butterscotch 22, 25,
    185, 321, 346, 385
  caramel 259
  chocolate 182
  chocolate hazelnut 264
  citrus 121
  custard 33
  fudge 248
  ginger 233
  ginger butterscotch 21
  golden syrup 369
  latte 377
  maple butterscotch 349
  mixed berry 252

(*sauce* continued)
  orange 361
  raspberry 201, 370
self-saucing puddings
  chocolate 256
  chocolate hazelnut 264
  chocolate, pear and
    hazelnut 248
  date and
    butterscotch 259
  ginger and orange 268
  hazelnut
    butterscotch 271
  jaffa 255
  lemon and mixed
    berry 252
  lemon delicious
    pudding 251
  microwave
    choc-cherry 263
  mocha, pear and
    nut 260
  orange and
    raspberry 272
  pineapple 267
semolina and yogurt
  lemon-syrup cake 345
soufflés
  apricot and honey 296
  black forest 287
  blackberry 312
  caramel soufflés with
    walnut praline 288
  chocolate 276
  chocolate liqueur 283
  coffee soufflés
    with pecan praline
    cream 300
  creamy marsala
    soufflés 291
  fresh apple 299
  frozen chocolate
    and coconut 280
  ginger 304
  hot chocolate soufflés
    with liqueur cream 279

(*soufflés* continued)
hot passionfruit
soufflé with
raspberry cream 315
hot raspberry 311
mango soufflés
with chocolate
collars 295
orange liqueur
soufflés with
macerated fruits 307
passionfruit 284
pear, red wine
and honey 303
pink grapefruit 316
rosewater 292
tangy lemon 308
spicy pumpkin and
hazelnut mousse 237
sponge cake 41
sponge topping 30
steamed puddings
chocolate and
golden syrup 185
chocolate hazelnut 186
chocolate bread
pudding with
brandy cream 178
chocolate chip 182
christmas 170
college 173
date 190
ginger 174
pumpkin and
maple pudding 181
quince and spice
steamed pudding
with orange syrup 189
tangelo syrup 177
sticky banana
macadamia pudding
with butterscotch
sauce 385
sticky date roll with
butterscotch
sauce 346

streusel 14
summer pudding 17
syrup 174, 177, 229
espresso 42
ginger 85
honey 102
lemon 345
lime 325
orange 189, 338
rum 366
vanilla 357
T
tangelo syrup pudding
177
timbale, coco-cherry
ice-cream timbale 109
tiramisu
hazelnut 98
individual 373
toffee date and
banana cake, upside
down 342
toffee date and ginger
puddings 21
trifle
chocolate and berry 54
classic 53
lemon curd, blueberry
and meringue 50
mango and lemon
chiffon trifle 62
peach and
raspberry trifle 61
raspberry and
chocolate mousse 58
tropical fruit 57
tropical fruit trifle 57
U
upside down toffee
date and banana
cake 342
V
vanilla panna cotta
with berry compote
133
vanilla syrup 357

W
walnut praline 288
white chocolate
see also chocolate
chocolate mousse
filling 205
white choc and
raspberry croissant
pudding 118
white chocolate
and black cherry
creamed rice 138
white chocolate
frozen christmas
pudding 110
white chocolate
mousse 202
white chocolate
panna cotta with
passionfruit sauce
126
Z
zabaglione, chocolate
245

conversion chart

MEASURES

One Australian metric measuring cup holds approximately 250ml, one Australian metric tablespoon holds 20ml, one Australian metric teaspoon holds 5ml.

The difference between one country's measuring cups and another's is within a two- or three-teaspoon variance, and will not affect your cooking results.North America, New Zealand and the United Kingdom use a 15ml tablespoon.

All cup and spoon measurements are level. The most accurate way of measuring dry ingredients is to weigh them. When measuring liquids, use a clear glass or plastic jug with the metric markings.

We use large eggs with an average weight of 60g.

LIQUID MEASURES

METRIC	IMPERIAL
30ml	1 fluid oz
60ml	2 fluid oz
100ml	3 fluid oz
125ml	4 fluid oz
150ml	5 fluid oz (1/4 pint/1 gill)
190ml	6 fluid oz
250ml	8 fluid oz
300ml	10 fluid oz (1/2 pint)
500ml	16 fluid oz
600ml	20 fluid oz (1 pint)
1000ml (1 litre)	1¾ pints

LENGTH MEASURES

METRIC	IMPERIAL
3mm	1/8in
6mm	1/4in
1cm	1/2in
2cm	3/4in
2.5cm	1in
5cm	2in
6cm	2½in
8cm	3in
10cm	4in
13cm	5in
15cm	6in
18cm	7in
20cm	8in
23cm	9in
25cm	10in
28cm	11in
30cm	12in (1ft)

DRY MEASURES

METRIC	IMPERIAL
15g	1/2oz
30g	1oz
60g	2oz
90g	3oz
125g	4oz (1/4lb)
155g	5oz
185g	6oz
220g	7oz
250g	8oz (1/2lb)
280g	9oz
315g	10oz
345g	11oz
375g	12oz (3/4lb)
410g	13oz
440g	14oz
470g	15oz
500g	16oz (1lb)
750g	24oz (1½lb)
1kg	32oz (2lb)

OVEN TEMPERATURES

These oven temperatures are only a guide for conventional ovens.
For fan-forced ovens, check the manufacturer's manual.

	°C (CELSIUS)	°F (FAHRENHEIT)	GAS MARK
Very slow	120	250	½
Slow	150	275 – 300	1 – 2
Moderately slow	160	325	3
Moderate	180	350 – 375	4 – 5
Moderately hot	200	400	6
Hot	220	425 – 450	7 – 8
Very hot	240	475	9

Published in 2010 by ACP Books, Sydney
ACP Books are published by ACP Magazines, a division of PBL Media Pty Limited

ACP BOOKS

General manager Christine Whiston
Editor-in-chief Susan Tomnay
Creative director & designer Hieu Chi Nguyen
Art director Hannah Blackmore
Senior editor Stephanie Kistner
Food director Pamela Clark
Recipe compiler Jordanna Levin
Sales & rights director Brian Cearnes
Marketing manager Bridget Cody
Senior business analyst Rebecca Varela
Operations manager David Scotto
Production manager Victoria Jefferys

Published by ACP Books, a division of ACP Magazines Ltd.
54 Park St, Sydney NSW Australia 2000. GPO Box 4088, Sydney, NSW 2001.
Phone +61 2 9282 8618 Fax +61 2 9267 9438
acpbooks@acpmagazines.com.au www.acpbooks.com.au

Printed by Toppan Printing Co., China.

Australia Distributed by Network Services, GPO Box 4088, Sydney, NSW 2001.
Phone +61 2 9282 8777 Fax +61 2 9264 3278
networkweb@networkservicescompany.com.au
United Kingdom Distributed by Australian Consolidated Press (UK),
10 Scirocco Close, Moulton Park Office Village, Northampton, NN3 6AP.
Phone +44 1604 642 200 Fax +44 1604 642 300
books@acpuk.com www.acpuk.com
New Zealand Distributed by Southern Publishers Group, 21 Newton Road, Auckland.
Phone +64 9 360 0692 Fax +64 9 360 0695 hub@spg.co.nz
South Africa Distributed by PSD Promotions, 30 Diesel Road Isando, Gauteng Johannesburg.
PO Box 1175, Isando 1600, Gauteng Johannesburg.
Phone +27 11 392 6065/6/7 Fax +27 11 392 6079/80 orders@psdprom.co.za
Canada Distributed by Publishers Group Canada
Order Desk & Customer Service 9050 Shaughnessy Street, Vancouver BC V6P 6E5
Phone (800) 663 5714 Fax (800) 565 3770 service@raincoast.com

Title: Puddings/food director Pamela Clark
ISBN: 978-1-86396-999-4 (pbk)
Subjects: Cookery (Puddings)
Other authors/contributors: Clark, Pamela
Also titled: Australian women's weekly
Dewey number: 641.864
© ACP Magazines Ltd 2010
ABN 18 053 273 546

To order books, phone 136 116 (within Australia) or **order online** at www.acpbooks.com.au
Send recipe enquiries to: recipeenquiries@acpmagazines.com.au

Front cover photographer Julie Crespel
Front cover stylist Louise Bickle
Front cover photochef Sarah Wilmot
Additional photography Julie Crespel, Dean Wilmot
Additional styling Louise Bickle
Photochefs Dominique Gekas, Elizabeth Macri, Amal Webster, Sarah Wilmot